Nurturing Your Child with Mentors

by
Craig Thompson

Published by Thompson Publishers

The Mentoring Revolution Series: Book Three

Thompson Publishers
https://thompsonpublishers.com

Nurturing Your Child with Mentors
The Mentoring Revolution Series: Book Three
Copyright © 2019 by Craig Thompson

Requests for information should be addressed to:
Thompson Publishers, PO Box 2605, Cleveland TN 37320-2605

ISBN: 978-1-64407-010-9 [softcover]
ISBN: 978-1-64407-011-6 [ebook]

All rights reserved. No part of this book may be reproduced, stored in a retrieval system, or transmitted in any form or by any means -- electronic, mechanical, photocopy, recording, or any other -- except for brief quotations printed in reviews, without the permission of the publisher.

Scripture taken from the New King James Version®. Copyright © 1982 by Thomas Nelson. Used by permission. All rights reserved.

Cover design Craig Thompson © 2019. Cover photo courtesy of Library of Congress. Reproduction of painting titled "Apprentice" by Emile Adan, 1914.

Printed in the USA.

"Paul wanted this young man
to journey with him."
Acts 16:3a

Other Books by the Same Author

The Mentoring Revolution Series
52 Godly Mentors Parent's Planning Guide

Asking for Wisdom: Maximizing Your Time with Mentors
This book is written for youth and is intended to teach them how to ask the kinds of question which will provide them with wisdom for living.

How To Be a Mentor for a Day
This book gives adults the tools they need to prepare for a successful day of mentoring. Included are steps for planning as well as thought-provoking questions which are useful in analyzing what parts of your life to share with a mentee.

The Mentoring Revolution Small Group Curriculum

Stories for Children
John and Gayle Stories

Other Works
Preaching Through Proverbs: A Collection of Sermons by the Pastors of Central Africa

Contents

Foreword
Our Story 1
Benefits of Being Mentored 4
Mentors Provide Opportunities 6
Mentors Convey Passion 12
Mentors Share Their Pain 17
Mentors Have Fun 24
Mentors Share Success Secrets 28
Mentors Shape Character 33
Mentors Offer a New Perspective 37
Mentors Teach Skills 41
Mentors Share Stories 51
Mentors Influence Spiritual Growth 57
Intentions Versus Intentionality 65
Examples of Mentors 68
Acknowledgements 93
About the Author 94
Comments 95
Errata 96

Foreword

No one ever said that raising children is easy. Homeschooling them is even harder. But once you discover a few secrets, the monumental task gets easier. One of those secrets is to engage appropriate mentors.

Throughout the 29 years my husband and I home educated our seven children, we found that associating our children with suitable mentors in a variety of subject areas had very positive effects on our children. Our oldest three children spent quite a bit of time with a stock market expert at his home. Our oldest son, starting at the age of 12, spent two days every week for two years at an auto mechanic's shop. Our second son spent several years working for and learning from a commercial and industrial roofer who lives five hours away. Our oldest daughter helped our next-door-neighbor bake marvelous cakes, which she sold and delivered to neighbors.

All of these experiences had such an impact in the lives of these children that today they are still reaping the rewards of time well spent. Two of the three oldest children continue to invest in the stock market. The son who spent time at the mechanic's shop now owns a trucking company where his knowledge of auto mechanics is quite useful. The son who mentored with the roofer owns a commercial and industrial roofing company in another state. The daughter who baked cakes worked in the bakeries of Walmart and Publix for many years.

Appropriate life experiences with seasoned mentors gives young people vision that can steer them in making vocational decisions. The secret is to find mentors who, first, exhibit excellent character and, second, skill. Luke 6:40 says that "everyone who is perfectly trained will be like his teacher"; and if parents allow their impressionable young people to be influenced by "experts" who lack character, they often will bring home the one trait or habit they shouldn't.

When Craig Thompson asked me to be one of the 52 Godly Women to spend time with Anna and then a few years later, Petra, I was honored. From the moment I heard about his concept, I loved it. I saw the wisdom in older people sharing part of their lives and their time with young people who are preparing themselves for the next stage of life. Feeling very inadequate about sharing something of value with Anna, I asked the Lord for a project. Just about that time, one of my oldest homeschool veteran friends, Pat Wesolowski, was hosting a one-day ladies' workshop at a camp featuring Nancy Campbell, publisher of Above Rubies magazine. So I asked Craig if he could drop Anna off at the camp to spend the day with all of us.

One lesson I wanted Anna to get from the experience was that no matter how old you are, you should always be learning from others. Nancy is an excellent teacher, and I knew she would speak words of wisdom for all of us to hear. Another lesson I wanted Anna to learn was that when one of your friends hosts an event, support her not only by telling others and going but also by taking someone with you. I wanted my friend Pat to have a good event, and I knew we would all enjoy spending the day together. More lessons came when I bought Anna a pile of Nancy's books to take home. First of all, because I have a home business, I could afford to make a financial investment in a marvelous young lady. I wanted her to see the rewards of having a home business. Second, Nancy's books contain important concepts that everyone needs to hear so I wanted Anna to have something very valuable to take home. Always take an expert – or their materials – home with you after you've experienced an amazing educational opportunity. Third, I wanted Anna to understand how much I value reading good literature. Successful people read. As the day went on, I took pictures of each aspect of the event and the friends we met. Once it was over, I had my card designer in Ohio, design and mail a greeting card to Anna for her to remember the day forever. The entire project felt successful to me.

A few years later, Craig asked me to spend some time with Petra. So once again, I asked the Lord, and He led us to work together as a vendor at a local homeschool convention. After all, the life of a vendor looks glamorous, but it's not. It's hard work. Craig's wife, Deana, dropped Petra off at the Chattanooga Homeschool Convention, where I've been teaching workshops on home business for more years than I can count, to spend the day in my booth. I took Petra with me to set up the computer in our workshop area and explained how to connect a laptop to an LCD projector and why a prepared speaker always brings things like their own clicker, an electric strip and an extension cord, whether they need them or not. I introduced her to Gary, the head of the event committee and had our picture taken with him. It's always good to meet people who make things happen. We discussed how to manage several sets of people in your booth at one time and that when you are manning a booth, it's not time to sit back and watch the people walk past, you're there to proactively serve them.

Petra got to spend some fun time shopping on the vendor floor and connected with some of her friends which is just one of the perks of attending professional events. After the event was over, Ms. Kathryn designed and mailed her a card with many of the pictures we took during the day.

Two sisters had two completely different experiences. In child training, I'm often surprised by parents who believe they should give their totally different children the exact same things – the same books, the same experiences, the same mentors. Sometimes that works. But most of the time it doesn't. Even though children may look very similar, they are usually very different. Tailoring their education to their individual personalities, skills, and needs is essential for them to mature into the productive adults we desire them to become.

That's why I am so excited that Craig Thompson is producing books and educational materials to share with others that explain what he has so successfully discovered with his own very wonderful children. I have personally been blessed by this man and his family and am thrilled that you are about to encounter an educational experience that will change your thinking and your life. In order to do that, you must forget what the world has taught you about training children and consider trying a mentoring project with your children.

This is wisdom from God. See it for what it is and don't let being too busy with "school" and life rob you of the benefits your family will gain from this concept. This is real education.

Rhea Perry
Educating for Success

Our Story

It was 3 a.m., and I was sick. I'm usually healthy, but something had gotten the best of me. As a result, I was sleeping a lot. But now, I was wide awake.

I'm the kind of guy that, if I'm going to be awakened at 3 in the morning, I might as well do something worthwhile. So, I sat in my chair thinking, meditating on questions and praying to God.

My son was turning 13 soon. Most adults realize that this age is a time of significant transition. For both boys and girls, this is the time when their bodies began to develop through the process of puberty. The chemicals in their bodies and brains pump rapid growth and change. In spite of this, most people I have known don't seem to have a plan for how to help their child navigate the rocky waters of this time of life.

I wanted something different for my son. For over a year, I had been trying to think of what to do to mark his passage from childhood into adulthood. A simple or elaborate ceremony such as a Bar Mitzvah didn't seem to meet the need. A big gift didn't seem to fit either. Even if I could have afforded it, what's a 13 year old going to do with a car or a boat or a motorcycle?

What I wanted was something which would be transformative, which would stretch out over time and which would help him grow as a person in some way. Originally, I had thought of having him meet with different business owners and entrepreneurs in order to learn from them the secrets of success in business. Yet, I couldn't shake the feeling that this idea wasn't it. It was incomplete.

So, sick but awake, I was praying for guidance. Like a stone dropped into a pond, the thought dropped into my mind, "52 GODLY men." Suddenly I was extra awake. I knew without a doubt that this was the answer I had been seeking. What I needed to give my son for his birthday was the opportunity to meet with men from all walks of life who were of noble character, men who would talk with him not just about business or money or investing, but who would share wisdom about life itself. I needed to find men who would help my son learn the importance of finding the right spouse, who would share their struggles and successes in raising children, who would talk about how their career choices impacted their lives on a daily basis, and who would help my son understand that making the right decisions over and over and over again would help him enjoy a wealth of success in every area of his life.

Once the idea was in my mind, it was illuminating. I began to write down name after name of men who I knew whom I wanted to spend time with my son. I began writing letters to them asking them if they would consider being part of a brand new project. And, as they responded, I began to schedule one man per week beginning with the week of my son's 13th birthday.

The rest is history. Well, to be frank, the rest was a lot of hard work. But since that time, I've had two daughters turn thirteen and complete the program. My fourth child is going through his own year of mentors. I've given them the same gift not just because they expected it or because I couldn't think of anything else. It's because I can't think of anything better to give to them.

The changes I have seen in each of their lives have been remarkable. In spite of the amount of time this gift takes to fulfill, at this point, I know it's worth every bit of time, energy, money and whatever effort is involved. My children have all grown enough to realize that what they received was priceless.

In this book, I would like to share some ideas with you about why you should find mentors for your children. You may be a parent, a grandparent, an aunt or uncle. You may be a teacher in a public school or a volunteer at a community youth organization. You may be a youth pastor. Regardless, I believe many of you reading this book already have a desire to do something more for those in your care, something which will propel them to greater heights and inspire them to new ideas.

As you read the chapters, think about the concepts and hear the stories from my children in their own words. We share them with you in order to help you grasp the importance of mentors. The success I have seen with my own children is not unique to my family. It is reproducible if you are willing to put forth the effort.

Benefits of Being Mentored

With a nine-year perspective on this program, I can say that all four of my children who have been through the program have been impacted in incredible ways. There have been numerous benefits, some of which I never foresaw. Before starting into the key principles found in the book, I wanted to give a big picture overview of just how powerful this type of program is for children. Here are just some of the positive things my wife and I have seen come from having our children meet with mentors on a regular basis:

- Better understanding of God's love
- Greater self-confidence
- Better interpersonal communication skills
- Ability to meet new people
- Ability and willingness to ask probing questions
- Enhanced critical thinking skills
- Better apprecation of how their education is preparing them for real life
- Personal maturation
- Integration with schooling (writing blogs, producing videos, writing books) reinforces the mentors' lessons
- Exposure to topics that parents forget
- Awareness about an issue or life challenge from the

viewpoint of someone who has lived it

- Relationship development which can pay off years into the future through job offers, referrals, prayers, or networking through friends of friends
- Opportunity to see different jobs and careers
- Chance to participate in unique experiences
- Learning that they can be mature, godly people without looking or thinking exactly like Dad or Mom
- Seeing how godliness and passion for Christ is lived out by others
- Learning to appreciate what they like about Dad and Mom even more
- Bonding times to/from appointments
- Gifts or mementos from mentors
- Appreciation of prayer and walking close to God
- Improved perception of how much the parent loves them
- Good memories with many mature adults
- Exposure to new cultures and new ways of doing things
- Formation of excitement in younger siblings as they hear what their older sibing is doing and learning
- Impact on siblings and others with lessons learned
- Improved writing skills from taking notes and/or writing reports about their mentoring meetings

Mentors Provide Opportunities

When I was a teenager, the World's Fair came to my region of the country. Because it was a once-in-a-lifetime event, my parents made the decision to visit it. I had never seen anything like it before and have seen very little like it since. All the major nations and quite a few of the others had exhibits. Without ever having been to China, I was able to see some of the actual pieces of the Terra Cotta Army of Qin Shi Huang which had recently been discovered. I was fascinated by the early introduction of robotics in manufacturing in the Japan exhibit. Then there was the brand new IMAX screen which was unveiled at that year's World's Fair. People were literally falling off their seats as they had a first-person view of a race car driving around mountain curves.

The wonderful part about it was that my family was no different from any other family. Anyone willing to pay the admission and endure the lines could attend the World's Fair.

There are, however, some experiences to which you and I will likely never be a party. I've never been invited to Buckingham Palace for a knighthood ceremony. Likewise, I have never gotten to visit the server room of the New York Stock Exchange or had a dinner in the Forbidden City. There are some experiences which you can have only if you have the right connections. Opportunities like these come from knowing someone who has an inside track to that location or the leaders over that experience.

Take the inner workings of a retail exposition or a curriculum fair, for instance. I've never worked one of them personally, but I know someone who has worked them numerous times. But before I say too much, I'll let Petra tell that story.

A Vendor's View of a Curriculum Fair

In the summer of 2017, I had the wonderful chance of meeting a woman of many talents, Rhea Perry. I was able to spend a day with her at a homeschool curriculum fair in Tennessee. Before that day, I had known of her but did not have a relationship with her. All that was about to change.

The day started when I first arrived at the convention. My mom had been to this fair numerous times and had always brought home stories of what was there, but I had never been and had no clue what to expect. As I walked through the double doors of the building, several people immediately greeted me. I signed in and was then given a name tag. As I walked into the arena, I was a little overwhelmed with all the booths and all the people. I knew Rhea had a specific table, but how in the world would I find it?

After walking around in circles for about ten minutes, I was finally able to locate the particular table. A lady who wasn't Rhea stood behind it. Puzzled, I introduced myself and found out that she was a travel agent, like Rhea, named Teresa Ball. She said that Rhea wasn't there presently but would be back shortly.

I decided to make myself familiar with the surroundings. There were tons of booths and tables all around me, and I really wanted to know just what went on at these fairs. I saw the expected schoolbooks and school supplies booths, but I also saw booths with educating card games, and a booth run by a dance studio. I was intrigued. My thoughts, though, were interrupted as I heard a voice calling my name.

I turned and found myself face to face with Rhea. I was happy to finally see her and couldn't wait to get started on a day full of adventures. She gave me a tour of the building, and I was finally able to locate the vital areas: the bathroom, the exit doors, and, most importantly, the private snack room filled with delicacies that a teenager like myself feast upon at midnight while poring over an enchanting novel. There were cookies and yogurt, muffins and Little Debbie's—as well as fruit and cheese, for all you healthy folks out there. I was told to "help myself," which I did so very willingly. But, I'm not here to talk about what I ate, right? I'm here to share with you readers about what I learned—although there is a lesson to be learned about never taking big bites right before you're about to talk with someone. After I swallowed, we were able to get to know each other better. I found out that she had homeschooled her kids and taught them many lessons as they grew up, and now they are successful entrepreneurs.

I have been homeschooled my whole life but hadn't thought of being an entrepreneur until a few years ago, when my dad, seeing that I had learned how to bake bread for my family, encouraged me to turn it into a business. This opened my eyes to a whole new world of possibilities. I then attended one of Rhea's conferences and learned that I, even at a young age, could make a business out of essentially anything. All I needed was a customer, an opportunity, and…oh! an idea. That's important to have.

After Rhea and I shared stories over snacks, we went to work. She had a workshop at 10:45 that she needed to prepare for. We walked into one of the enclosed areas where the workshop was going to be held, and she taught me how to set up for a presentation, knowledge I can now use in the future. We set up her computer and the projector and plugged everything in. Nothing happened. I was starting to grow nervous. We tried again, with the same results. Finally, a man—who had walked in a bit early and was sitting on the front row—asked if he could give it a try. With his help, and God's, the projector and computer were able to work together. I sat in the back as people began to stream in. At the start of the workshop, Rhea told the large group the goal for her business: to help parents educate their children and to encourage them to discover what they love and use that to start a business. She shared some stories about her successful children, keeping the audience enthralled with her fun-loving nature. Once she had finished her workshop, she told everyone to grab a package about her conference in August on their way out. I had a large stack of them in my hand, but I soon realized I hadn't gotten enough. I dashed back to the booth to grab more and was able to make it back to the workshop area before too many people had left. After the last person had left, Rhea and I walked back to her booth.

We were able to talk with some people who wanted to know more about Educating For Success, the name of the business she runs. Some were only there a few minutes before dashing off, but others stayed hours to talk and get to know Rhea better, which I don't blame them for. She is an incredible woman of many talents, strengths, and ideas.

As lunch drew near, we ate barbecue sandwiches provided by the fair. I was hungry, despite my over-indulgence in flavored yogurt. I learned from her over lunch that you don't learn to think creatively by following the rules; you learn by trying and failing multiple times. It made me want to try harder to do that—defy all odds and try and fail until I succeed.

I was able to watch her interact with all the people who came by and wondered how she could always have a smile ready and just the right information for just the right person. All too soon, however, our time together was brought to an end when the fair closed for the day and we packed up only the necessary items, taking them to her car. I hadn't even realized how late it had gotten, but, sure enough, night was falling as we headed to a restaurant. Two other women joined us, one of whom was Teresa, the woman I had met before. We made light talk until my ride came to pick me up.

All in all, I was able to experience things with Rhea I had never experienced before in my life. She inspired me to look for new venues in the business world and to take my current business further. And hopefully by reading about this amazing woman named Rhea Perry, you will have been inspired, too.

Dad's Thoughts
Rhea didn't spend all of her time that day with Petra. But that wasn't her role. What she was willing to do was to open up a door of opportunity for Petra which I could not open by myself. Because of that, my child experienced what it is like to set up and prepare for a retail vendor exposition. She learned some of what goes on behind the scenes. She saw some of the hard work that makes events happen.

The other children have had similar opportunities through

some of the mentors they met. David met with a concert promoter who gave him an "All Access" pass from 10 a.m. until after midnight. He got to see the set up and preparation which goes into making a concert happen. Along the way, he met some of the performers and was even invited to check out their tour bus.

Anna had the opportunity to spend a day with a professional ballet troupe as they prepared for a dress rehearsal of a major production. She did warm-up exercises with them and also participated in their classes as they honed their techniques. Then, in the evening, she was able to see the cast work through the scenes of the performance.

Paul has gotten to work on a live renovation site by spending time with a mentor who runs a construction business. He not only learned about the history of the mentor's growth in business but he also was able to rip out walls and sheetrock as they prepared to add new living space in an attic. For a child who loves to work with his hands, this was sheer pleasure for him.

Sometimes it's not about the words that are spoken or about any particular lesson shared by a mentor. Sometimes it's just about the opportunity to be there for yourself.

Mentors Convey Passion

Some of the men I remember from my childhood are the itinerant preachers who would visit my church and hold meetings for a week or more. We called them evangelists. Whatever their name, they were mostly a pretty wild bunch. There was a certain style which most of them followed. They wore suits and ties, had well groomed hair (at least until the preaching started) and exhibited an exuberance which was unparalleled. One thing which impressed me even as a child was how passionate they were. They were determined to save souls even if it were the last thing on earth they would do.

How many people do you know who actually live with such passion? Life has a way of grinding us down. People put their head down, go to work, raise their family, endure the brunt of life and forget the things which they dreamed about as kids.

Well, not everyone. There are some people who still live with passion. When they get up, they know that their work is going to make a difference in the world, and they savor that. I've been able to find a few of those people for my children. I'll let Anna tell her story first.

Saving Innocent Lives
Many of the women I met with during my 52 Godly Women experience were passionate about a wide variety of matters. However, a woman I met with one day gave me an inside view of life, death, and the choice in between. I met with Tracie Shellhouse, the director of New Hope

Pregnancy Center, a non-profit, pro-life clinic that offers help to girls who are thinking about seeking an abortion.

New Hope's main mission is to lead girls down the right path for choosing life for their babies while sharing the Gospel with them. The clinic also gives post-abortion counseling, with no condemnation, for those who have chosen an abortion in the past. Yet, they don't stop there. They also give help, recourses, and supplies for girls and women in need. Tracie told me, "Many of the girls coming in are hoping for a negative test. For many of them, marriages will be broken, girls will be thrown out of their family homes, and some will even be disowned by their families if they choose life."

It is surprising, though, that many of the girls who walk through their doors profess to be Christians. When Tracie asks a girl if she knows the Lord, many times she'll get the response, "I go to church sometimes," or, "I used to pray." She shared with me that a man or woman going to church a few times a year makes them a Christian just as much as standing in their garage makes them a car—it doesn't. Being a Christian involves a relationship with Jesus, not with the pew they sit on. Most people just want the "Jesus inoculation." This is a term given to the people who say, "Give me just enough of Jesus to be as messed up as everyone else." Instead, a true relationship with Jesus will make a person say, "I will never be satisfied with my relationship with Jesus until I get to Heaven." Although the girls walking into their clinic profess Christianity, Tracie walks them through the gospel again and opens their pain-laden eyes to God's love.

Tracie shared with me many abortion statistics. But what I found the most interesting (or maybe I should say appalling) is that a doctor can kill the "fetus" when it is only three inches in the womb, but if he slips up and the baby comes down three inches into the world, the doctor could be sued for murder! It is all right to kill the "blob" inside the womb, but outside the womb it is considered murder? That doesn't add up.

As well, Tracie often gets asked, "Is that fetus really a baby?" She humorously responds, "I've never heard of a woman having puppies before! Have you?" However, when you get to the base of this argument, it is about what time life actually starts. Think about it, though. When is the moment that everyone knows a baby is alive? Most people can agree that a baby is alive the day it was born. However, is that baby any less alive the day before that? Or how about the day before that? Tracie told me, "Life starts at conception. Even at week nine the baby's eye color and hair color have already been determined!" Why? Because life doesn't start the day it's born; it starts when God puts a child inside a woman and says, "This is a gift from me to you."

A woman becomes bonded to her child even at the early stages of life because those nine months of pregnancy were designed for a time of bonding. When girls receive an abortion, they believe it's a good idea at first, but then depression and anxiety skyrocket off the charts. Tracie shared with me another statistic: eighty percent of the women behind bars have had an abortion, which then caused them to start making worse decisions for their lives.

Maybe in America at this moment abortion is ok, legally, but when you look at all of the side effects and the decision of killing a baby that can never be undone, erased, or forgotten, abortion is a terrible moral and ethical crime.

The time I spent with Tracie opened my eyes to a world I had been oblivious to. So many girls are weighed down with the fear of choosing life or the guilt from choosing an abortion. And although there are many voices who claim to the girls that an abortion is harmless and safe, it seems that the voices who share the emotional damage abortions have caused are scattered and few in number. I learned that day that life starts at conception and that there are people out there like Tracie Shellhouse and her team at New Hope Pregnancy Center who offer support and resources for women and girls who are considering an abortion. What I learned that day has stayed with me all of these years, and it has allowed me to share with others the importance of choosing life.

Dad's Thoughts
Our home is a pro-life home. We emphasize to our children the value of life in numerous ways as they grow up. We don't promote the voices which would advocate the killing of an innocent child, the sick, the mentally challenged or an aged adult.

But when Anna met with Tracie, she got a huge dose of Tracie's passion injected into her heart and mind. Years later after meeting with 52 different godly women, Tracie still ranks in the top five women whom Anna enjoyed meeting with. Why? It's because you can't be around someone like Tracie for long without being infected by her contagious passion for saving lives.

Who do you know who can impact your child in this way? What level of passion do they have? And do they have a passion for something which you want your child to catch? If you don't put godly mentors in their path, the ungodly ones are just as passionate about their causes, and they will do their best to impact the heart and mind of your child.

Tracie has met with two of my daughters now. Both of them list her as one of their favorite mentors to meet with. The reason is simple: she is passionate about what she does, and she exudes that when she spends time with others. Because Tracie and other mentors were willing to spend time with my children, they were impacted at a deep level. They got to see the passion which drives these men and women every day.

Do you think that passion can rub off on others? I've seen it happen. Any time I can add more fuel to my children's fire for living life fully, I'm going to do it. People with passion change the world. I want my children to learn from them and become one of them.

Mentors Share Their Pain

Spiritual gurus, whether they are Christian, Hindu, Buddhist or any other flavor have at times been guilty of a heinous crime. They have told their followers, "Believe what I am telling you, and all of your problems will go away." It doesn't matter what you believe, life can be hard as flint, and life has a way of smashing erroneous theologies to pieces.

But what do you do when your belief system fails? What happens when really good people go through the worst kinds of pain? I'm not interested in the people who fall apart and run to alcohol, drugs, violence or other type of harmful choices when trouble hits. Anyone can do those things, and time proves that those are wrong decisions. The question is, how do people of character endure suffering?

When I look for mentors for my children, I try to purposefully look for some people who have gone through the fire and come out the other side stronger. Here is the sad but hopeful story of one of the men who met with David.

Character Assassination
"Curse God and die." That was the advice the biblical figure of Job got from his wife after he lost his kids, his stuff, and even his health. Of course, God wasn't the one doing all of this to Job; Satan was, with God's permission. However, when faced with the total extinction of everything he held dear, Job wasn't focused on technicalities. What Job did focus on, though, was the same thing he had fallen back on every time another catastrophe hit: his faith. In the

face of human nature, his friends, and even his family, Job remained faithful to God, even when given an easy way out: to curse God and let it all end. Job's choice between profanity and piety is the same choice that was presented to the man I met with during my mentoring journey, Pastor Jason Fitzgerald. [Editor's note: name changed for privacy purposes.]

Both Jason's father and grandfather were also preachers. As a result, Jason was well acquainted with things like faith, prayer, and other Christian principles while he was still young. After becoming a pastor, Jason's faith helped him through several stormy patches in his ministry, starting at the very beginning. His first "church" was really a movie theater, chairs and choir robes not provided. They had to be out of the theater completely by 1:00 p.m. every Sunday, and you know how hard it is for church people to stop socializing! However, Jason kept faithfully leading his congregation, and eventually, they saved up enough money to build a brand new church on almost 20 beautiful acres of land.

Jason's next spiritual test came a little while after the transition. Apparently, the brand new building and the beautiful land had caught someone's eye, because some people in the denomination he was a part of (which shall remain nameless and thus blameless) conspired against him and tried to take the property away—even though Jason and his congregation personally paid for the whole thing. Legally. And built a church on it. It took two whole years in court for the whole affair to get straightened out, but at long last, Jason won the case and the church was able to keep the property. But don't feel bad for the people who tried to do him dirty. If they really wanted a church that badly, I hear there's still a movie theater available on Sundays. Just be out before 1:00 p.m.

Jason continued to pastor his church for many years. His ministry grew, God blessed him, and the days of standing in court were behind him, or so it seemed. Then, in January of 2005, Jason had his biggest test of faith yet. His world came crashing down; he got the rug pulled out from under him; the bottom dropped out; he took one on the chin; look, pick an analogy, but just understand it was BAD! Two policemen came to the church asking for Jason Fitzgerald, and when Jason went outside with them, two plainclothes officers slapped him in cuffs and carted him off to jail. After ten minutes of asking in vain why he was in the back of a police car, one officer finally broke the news to Jason. He had been accused of molesting a relative's child.

There are good surprises, like finding out you're going to an amusement park for vacation instead of staying home with your aunt. There are also bad surprises, like when your monthly power bill is twice as high as usual and you were planning on using that extra money to buy a new television. And then there's being told you're a child molester, by a policeman, on your way to jail, with no clue how any of this happened. This was a very bad surprise indeed, and for Jason, things were only about to get worse.

When Jason arrived at the police station, he was convinced there was just some mistake and he would be able to clear up the confusion in a few minutes. That didn't happen. Instead, Jason spent five hours in an interrogating room, repeatedly pleading his innocence to disbelieving officers convinced of his guilt. Needless to say, the interrogation did not go well for either party. After the policemen finally ended the cross-examination, they slapped Jason in a holding cell until they could find a better place to put him. The place was so filthy he had to stand up the whole time he was in it. And he was in it for two days.

Jason finally got out of the holding cell, but his situation only got worse. On his way to the jail, a guard gave him some friendly advice: "Some of the prisoners you'll be around were molested as children, so be careful, because convicted felons tend to hold grudges." Comforting words indeed. When he arrived at the jail, Jason met his cellmates. One guy was arrested for serious battery charges, and the other one was accused (and eventually convicted) of murder. Not the type of people Pastor Jason was used to living with, and certainly not the pair he would have voluntarily picked to be around for the indefinite future.

Let's pause the story right here and reflect. Someone, we don't know who, falsely accused Jason, a pastor of a thriving church, of molesting an underage relative. He was then promptly arrested, interrogated, thrown in a holding cell, and eventually locked in jail with a murderer as a cellmate. This was the point where Jason encountered the same choice that landed in the lap of Job. Option one: stay faithful and positive, keep being a godly influence, forgive the person who accused you of heinous and unspeakable crimes, and ignore the negative kickback you'll receive from your congregation if you ever get out of jail. Option two: curse God and (hopefully) die. Option two would have been quick, easy, and wouldn't have required any more effort from Jason than saying "hello" to a neighbor. No muss, no fuss, no worrying about proving his innocence or dealing with the ramifications of being labeled a sex offender or serving hard time in jail or watching his congregation suffer and eventually leave. I bet option two looked really enticing in the moment. But when Jason had nothing else, when there was no one to defend him, he fell back on the one thing that had lifted him above every major obstacle he had ever overcome: his faith.

Instead of letting his heart harden and giving up on God, Jason praised God and embraced his calling. He began ministering to his cellmates and later to the other prisoners as well. He stayed faithful and kept believing that God had a plan for him, even in the darkest place possible. At Jason's bail hearing, one of the arresting officers who had also helped interrogate him provided false information that differed from his testimony and the fact of the arrest, just to keep Jason from being released on bail. However, his family and several members of his church testified in his favor, and the judge set a $50,000 bond. Shortly afterward, another man from Jason's congregation pledged his home for bond so Jason could be released!

Jason was locked up for nineteen days, and he spent each one of them ministering to the inmates. Before he left the jail, the guard over his cellblock brought all of the other prisoners out of their cells and every one of them prayed for him. That's the kind of impact Jason had on them. Had he chosen the easy way out and given up, none of those men would ever have heard the message of the gospel or seen the power of one man's faith.

For Jason's trial, his wife found a lawyer who only dealt with child abuse cases, and he hired two retired FBI agents to help with the case. They photographed everything in his house, looking for some piece of evidence that could help his cause. They asked him to take a lie detector test so they would know he was innocent—which Jason promptly agreed to without question—and he not only passed, but he got the highest score the administering agent had ever seen and didn't tell a single lie!

The prosecution had no evidence against Jason. He passed every test they administered with flying colors, but it took fifteen months for the prosecution to drop the charges. Despite the many harrowing months Jason spent in limbo, though, and despite the villainous things he was accused of, he was still able to forgive the people who treated him so badly. His faith in God was paramount throughout the whole experience, as evidenced by what Jason told me: "I wouldn't trade that experience for anything. How can I look back at that time and doubt that God was with me?"

I have five siblings, and I would be repulsed if I were to be accused of sexually abusing a child I'm related to. I don't know what I'd do if I were actually prosecuted for such a disgusting act. But I do know what Jason Fitzgerald did, and I know how he did it. He kept his faith in God, even in the face of unspeakable evil, and much like Job, he came out of his trial better than he entered it. He was given a choice: walk the hard road through your tribulation, or curse God and die. By faith and through prayer, Jason continued to praise.

Dad's Thoughts
In the story above, an innocent man's life and career was damaged by a lie. Due to the seriousness of the charge (even though it was false), some people will never trust him again in spite of his innocence. That's wrong. Yet, history is full of examples of people who were slandered and punished unjustly, even to the point of death.

Many of the people who have met with my children have

undergone really challenging situations in their lives. Some people in similar situations would have turned bitter, but these mentors turned out better. I have told my children, "I hope you never have to go through the same tough life situations that some of your mentors have. But if you ever do, I want you to have met and talked with people who have done it before you so you will know that you, too, can make it." When you find mentors who are willing to share their pain, you are educating your children about the reality of suffering while still showing them the keys to how to endure it.

Mentors Have Fun

After a chapter on suffering, it's a good balance to talk about the importance of enjoying life. The family I grew up in knew how to have fun. Our parents taught us about hospitality and how to enjoy life, even on a budget. We played all kinds of games both indoors and outdoors. We invited numerous friends and whole families over for meals, fellowship and recreation. Since growing up, we have each tried to pass that along to our children. But, as with everything else, mentors can bring a new perspective on ways to do that.

My daughter Petra loves to bake. My wife actually found one of her mentors while searching for a list of Christian bakers in our area. I made the appointment, but I'll let Petra tell you her story of meeting with Shona House.

Baking with Purpose
In late September, my dad and I made a two-hour drive up to Rogersville, TN so I could meet with a baker named Shona House. We climbed out of the car and stretched. I then suddenly came to the annoying realization that I had forgotten my notebook. It was too late to turn back, so when we knocked on her door and met Shona, I asked if she had some paper I could use. She did, of course, and let me use it willingly.

Once my dad had left, Shona and I started to get to know one another. She owns her own bakery called "Faith Baked Cakes," is the proud mother of two grown boys, Landon and Justin, and has a testimony that proves God is faithful.

The day before her son Landon's high-school graduation,

Justin, Shona and her husband were driving on the interstate when they had a major car accident. Their truck rammed against fence posts, making the truck flip. Her husband died, and her son was severely injured. Despite the fact that she was injured as well, she never stopped praying for her family; and her prayers were answered. Justin—whose lungs and kidneys were punctured, had 390 stitches, and overall had an 8% chance of survival—was released from the hospital one week after the accident.

Now, what you may not know about Shona is that if she has a mind to do something, she does it. This proved to be a problem when the day after the accident she insisted on seeing Landon graduate. The hospital staff wasn't at ease with that idea, to say the least. But because of her driven nature, she was released for a short time to attend his graduation. The whole town stood and clapped for Landon as he walked across the stage because people had heard of the family's accident and wanted to show their support.

After the death of her husband, Shona didn't have a stable income. She had been given a vision about a cake shop being built, but she wanted to wait, plus she had to figure out how to come up with enough money to get Landon through college and to keep herself and Justin alive. God kept telling her to build it, but she wouldn't listen. Finally, she gave up fighting. She gave God the reins.

As a result, God provided people to donate building materials for her shop, people to help build the shop, and people to give her the equipment needed to furnish the shop. Pretty soon, she found herself with a shop built onto the side of her house. God had done so many miraculous things in her life—including allowing her to live.

Once she had told me her story—and I sat there fully amazed at God's provision—she and I started to decorate cakes. She already had the cake layers made; we were just going to decorate them together. She showed me how to crumb and ice a cake, and I did the best I could under the circumstances—I had never really done anything with cakes before, other than eat them.

Once the double-tiered cake was ready, we decided on an ocean theme for the decoration. She brought out several tubs of different-colored fondant. We chose a dark blue and a lighter blue fondant to roll together so it would make a swirled pattern, like waves. Then we put it on the cake and made sure there were no rips in the fondant or wrinkly places.

With an ocean cake, there had to be some sea creatures in it, right? We solved that problem as we made little fish, seashells, a mermaid, a jellyfish, a treasure chest, and some seaweed. As the big bang for the finish, we added a ginormous, pink octopus made partially out of Rice Krispies to the top of the cake, with its tentacles hanging down over all sides. It looked magnificent.

After that cake, I also was able to crumb and ice another cake for a customer. I had a lot of fun seeing my slight improvement between the first and second times I decorated the different cakes. She then made us grilled sandwiches with homemade lemonade for lunch, which I ate up quickly. Just then, my dad knocked on the screen door of her shop. She placed my cake in a box so I could easily transport it home, and then said goodbye. I thanked her for her time with me and headed out to the car carrying a large, blue cake in my hands.

As my dad and I drove home, I reminisced about my meeting. She had not only gifted me with the ability to know how to make a cake and not look like a crazy person, but she had also shared with me the all times that God provided for her and took care of her and her family, which made my faith stronger.

Dad's Thoughts

Petra heard someone's story of victory coming out of suffering. But in spite of the heavy nature of Shona's story, Petra had an incredibly enjoyable day. When I picked her up, she was bubbling over with story after story both of what she had learned from Shona and of what she had done with her. That kind of joy is priceless. When you find mentors who can bring that kind of joy to your children, you are teaching them that it's possible to have fun without resorting to harmful behavior, bad decisions or any regrets.

When you look for mentors, it's a good idea to find some people who know how to have good, clean fun. Whether it's a sport, a hobby or a skill, your child's time with that person can awaken an interest, fuel a lifelong interest or result in a career. Plus, the life lessons they learn from the mentors during those fun outings sink in for a long time.

Mentors Share Success Secrets

When I was a child, I loved to read books. I remember reading a story about two boys who lived in the same apartment building in the city. For some reason, they didn't like each other at first sight, and they treated each other poorly. One day, one of the boys was trying to fly a kite without a tail. The second boy remarked that he might be able to actually fly it if he would put a tail on it. Another time, the second boy was trying to hammer a nail into a cart he was making, but he was holding the hammer by the neck. The first boy commented that he might be able to hammer without bending all the nails if he would hold the hammer by the end of the handle. In the story, they each tried the other's idea, and when it worked, they became friends.

I remember building a barn one time. We did some of the work ourselves, but when it came time to put on the roof, we had a carpenter come in and help with the rafters. It was amazing to see all the tricks of the trade he knew which made putting those rafters up not only much safer but also much simpler. As I watched him, I learned quite a bit about how to put a roof on a barn. Success in learning how to put on a barn roof was not impossible for me to attain; I just needed someone who knew the secrets of that success.

Every good mentor knows something. It may be about money, it may be about automobiles, it may be about cooking, music, raising triplets or any number of other topics. When I look for mentors for my children, I try to include people who are experts in a given field or have a wealth of experience to share.

My son, Paul, had an opportunity to be in the first-ever mentoring group for youth at our church using the curriculum I've written. We had men from our church come and speak each week to the boys. There were a wide array of stories, lessons and wisdom which these men shared. Some of the men had strong bullet points on topics related to success. Paul worked through his notes to share the following keys to success with you.

Keys to Success in Business

When Jake Radcliff (name changed for privacy) spoke to our mentoring group, he shared some of his secrets to success in business. Here is his list, along with some of the thoughts he shared about each one:

1. Make friendships early in life; they will help you later on in life. Jake had started a friendship with an older man. By spending time with him, such as going out to lunch, he built the friendship. About ten years later, he started working for this man and later bought the man's business from him, providing him with a steady income.

2. Work hard. Jake actually had one experience where he drove about 700 miles just to deliver three small boxes of candy for a taste test for one of the local candy manufacturers. If you work hard, you will receive favor from your boss.

3. Research what you want to do. Jake said you have to know what you are doing before you begin doing it, or most likely you will fail.

4. Show up every day. If you show up every day, your boss

will notice it and will (probably) give you a raise. Don't make excuses as to why you cannot be at work.

5. Be flexible in your work schedule. You should work, but you should also make time for your family. Your family is more important than your work, no matter how much money you make.

6. Be willing to get out of your comfort zone. An example of this might be a baseball player, who is comfortable hitting from his dominant hand side of the plate, switching to the other side of the plate. It would be a challenge, but it could also result in positive growth.

What I learned from Jake by listening to him speak is the importance of making as many good relationships as you can and to know your business.

Traits of Healthy Relationships

Another person who came and spoke to our group was Martin Balfour (name changed for privacy). He talked about Traits of Healthy Relationships. Here are Martin's points along with some details on each:

1. Understanding.

2. Trust. Martin said that you must be able to trust your wife, your friends, your employees and others. If you cannot trust people, your relationships will fall apart.

3. Honesty. You must be honest, or else your life will become darker as time passes, and this will show through in your attitude.

4. Values. You must be able to value your family and relationships more than your work or material possessions.

5. Respect. If you do not respect other people, people will not want to be around you.

6. Risk. You have to be willing to risk your life, your career, and other things which matter to you in order to save or to serve your family.

7. Breaking down barriers. Martin worked in Afghanistan. During that time, he had two bodyguards who were Muslim. Still, they built a relationship in spite of the language barrier, the cultural barrier, and the religious barrier. Eventually, those two men died giving their lives for Martin.

8. Commitment. If your friends are going through a hard time, you have to be willing to make time to help them. Commitment means being willing to hang out with people.

9. Ability to listen. Martin's father lost most of his hearing in the military. Whenever his wife would start to get in an argument with him, he would just take out his hearing aids. People who didn't know about this tactic asked him how he could sit so quietly with a peaceful expression on his face. However, listening sometimes means being able to put up with hearing things you may not wish to hear.

10. Love. Martin said that you must be able to love your wife (and other people) even when it is very hard.

11. Continuing to learn. You must be open to learning even in areas in which you struggle or have no interest. Continue to talk to and listen to others in order for your relationships to keep growing stronger.

Overall, what I learned from Martin is the importance of relationships. Listening to him made me want to hang out with my friends more so that I could get to know them better.

Dad's Thoughts

When you read through a list like that, it's impressive. Paul was eleven years old when he sat with other middle school boys and heard these men share these points. While I don't expect him to remember all of them by heart, the fact is, he does remember some of these points without having to look at his notes. In a larger perspective of meeting with multiple mentors, some of these lessons will get hammered home multiple times until they become part of his way of thinking.

The information above is only a partial list of all the lessons the children have been exposed to through the many meetings with their mentors. The point is, the lessons of success are out there waiting to be taught, and the children are also there waiting to learn. Seek mentors who are experts so that your child can learn the secrets of success early in life.

Mentors Shape Character

One day after I was already an adult and had been in business, I had a conversation with my accountant. We were talking about some of the things I liked to do and the ways I liked to create new services. He looked at me and said matter-of-factly, "You're an entrepreneur." When he spoke those words, it was like being fitted for a pair of eyeglasses for the first time. Everything snapped into focus. I realized that I had certain tendencies, gifts and abilities, but to have someone describe me that way actually made sense to me in a brand new way.

Nothing had changed about me personally, but I saw myself differently after that. I realized that the way I am is a gifting from God in order to create opportunities not only for myself and my family but also for others. I was more open to embracing those gifts and developing them rather than seeing them as a hindrance to life.

That's what a mentor can do. Over the course of time, meeting with one or more mentors can help bring into focus your child's gifts and talents and allow them to understand their value. It may be the same truth you've been trying to get your child to see, but sometimes hearing the same thing from a new person makes all the difference. That happened on several occasions with each of my children. For this story, I'll let Petra relate the details.

Servanthood
I believe that out of all the women I've met with, my aunt Charissa Smith has shaped my character the most. When

I met with her, I didn't know I was going to walk away completely changed. I had met with 28 women before her, so it wasn't like there was anything special about the number. Despite my expectations, I ended up learning a great deal.

We met up in a coffee shop. I personally love coffee shops that aren't super well known because a lot of the time they're the best, the coziest, and the cheapest. She started off the conversation by informing me that the theme of the day was going to be servanthood. In fact, she believed that was one of the most important qualities in a godly woman.

That used to be an iffy subject with me. It's not like I wouldn't hold open the door for someone if they needed help or do some kind deed every once in a while, but to become a slave to everyone around me? Not my type. However, I didn't really understand what I was required to do as a servant. After meeting with Aunt Charissa, I have a much better idea of what true servanthood is about.

The Bible has a lot to say on the subject. Check out Colossians 3:23-24, "And whatever you do, do it heartily, as to the Lord and not to men, knowing that from the Lord you will receive the reward of the inheritance; for you serve the Lord Christ."

Aunt Charissa told me that we're servants of the King; so, when we serve others, we are also serving Christ, just like Colossians says. Jesus is the ultimate example for servanthood. The Bible tells us in Matthew 20:2, "Just as the Son of Man did not come to be served, but to serve, and to give His life a ransom for many."

Think about it! Jesus spent His last few hours before he

died serving His disciples by washing their feet. Now, you may have a strange attraction to feet, but as for me, I think that's pretty gross. It's hard for me to even smell dirty feet, much less rub them, and yet that act of servitude was one of the last things Jesus did before He died. He loves us so much that He would do any type of service to bring us back to Him.

In fact, Christ's unconditional love is our motivation for serving others. Philippians 2:5-8 says, "Let this mind be in you which was also in Christ Jesus, who, being in the form of God, did not consider it robbery to be equal with God, but made Himself of no reputation, taking the form of a bondservant, and coming in the likeness of men. And being found in appearance as a man, He humbled Himself and became obedient to the point of death, even the death of the cross."

Aunt Charissa said that nothing disciplines our flesh as much as serving because there is no task that is below you when you're a servant. She noted that you shouldn't wait until you feel an obvious push from God to serve, but instead, do it when you know it needs to be done, no matter whether God wrote it in black and white for you or not.

And while being a servant, you can't just sit on a shelf and look pretty. You have to get sweaty and dirty while still having a good attitude. You have to be durable, not dainty. 2 Timothy 2:20 says, "But in a great house there are not only vessels of gold and silver but also of wood and clay, some for honor and some for dishonor." You need to be like a clean mug ready for daily use, rather than like a dainty china teacup or a Christmas dish—things that are rarely used. As Bill Hybels put it, "I would never want to reach out someday with a soft, non-calloused hand—a hand never dirtied by serving—and shake the nail-pierced hand of Jesus."

If you haven't yet felt as if this chapter is for you, then that should kick you right in the gut. If Jesus served us in the most painful way possible, then why would we push off small, simple acts for later? It could be as easy as sweeping a dirty floor without being asked to take a load off your Mom's mind, doing a chore for a sibling who's swamped with homework, or taking some time out of your day to spend some quality time with your kids. Whatever it is, know that Jesus is smiling down on you for what you are doing, even if no one else knows. Matthew 6:3 tells us, "But when you give to the needy, do not let your left hand know what your right hand is doing." If no one gives you a pat on the back for something you did, don't worry! You'll be rewarded in heaven from God more than you'd ever get on Earth from humans. So take a moment, think about something you could do, and do it! Don't hesitate and think that you probably have something more important going on, or you'll miss the moment.

Dad's Thoughts

In this example, a mentor spoke a truth at a key time. That, combined with a willingness to listen, produced a positive change in my child's life. Can you control what lessons will be learned at what time? Usually not. However, you can arrange for your child to meet with mentors and can help to create the environment in which those lessons can be taught. Over the course of time, some of those lessons may turn out to be the key to unlock your child's understanding and propel him to great growth.

Mentors Offer a New Perspective

If you ever travel to Great Britain, you should sit down at a restaurant and observe how the locals hold their forks. I was raised to hold a fork with the tines bending up. Imagine that there's a whole country where people hold their forks with the tines pointing down. I tried it myself. I was amazed to find that eating certain foods became much more convenient simply by turning the fork over.

Have you ever had that experience of doing something one way your whole life and then discovering that there's a different — maybe a better way — of doing it? Probably right now all the married people are thinking about how different their spouse did common things after they got married. But it's the differences which can cause us to ponder our own ways of doing things. Mentors who have totally different careers, interests and education bring a brand new perspective to your children, one which you can never bring yourself.

Anna had several mentors who took her out of her comfort zone. I'll let her tell you what she learned from one of them.

From Gang to God
Growth happens when a perspective is shifted. In my case, my perspective of good kids, bad kids, and single moms was shifted in a very direct direction when I met with Evie West. Evie grew up in a strong, Christian household with

loving parents and attended Christian schools. However, when her parents couldn't pay for her to go to private schools anymore, Evie started out her high school years in a public, Los Angeles high school. Right away she realized that the gangs in the school were tough, and after getting beat up and surviving it, she got sucked into wanting to be just like them. She started off slowly, dabbling with what would soon suck her into a life she would have never thought possible.

Evie started to act, talk, and even walk like the kids who were popular in her school, even bullying like them. She started to earn their respect, but she wanted more. After a compromising night at fourteen years old, she pushed herself deeper into the streets of Los Angeles and rebelled even more against her heartbroken parents and everything she had ever learned from the Bible. At the age of sixteen, with a boyfriend in her life, she was given the title of a full-fledged gang member after a merciless initiation. Yet because of her deception, her parents were still not aware of what was fully happening. Daily she ran the risk of getting killed multiple times, but after having a gun pointed to her face and living to tell the story, she realized that her life needed to change.

Evie left to go with a group on a mission trip to the Dominican Republic where there were no gangs, just her and God. She started reading the Bible and during that time in her life she kept hearing God say, "I love you." Evie called her boyfriend to tell him she couldn't see him anymore and was on the path back to a right lifestyle. She was changing. When she got back, she started seeing a pastor's son who had been a very good friend for a long time. She even shared her testimony with his dad's congregation on how much Jesus had changed her life. Soon afterwards, however, she found out that she was pregnant from her previous relationship. People jeered, her parents cried, and her Christian boyfriend dropped her.

Evie was confused. She wondered why God would let this happen, why He had let her down. So after she gave birth to her son, she began hanging out with her old gang members. Night-after-night Evie made her parents her personal babysitters, and yes, entered into a new relationship with another gang member. One night her mom had had enough and told Evie to leave with her son to start a new life.

When Evie moved to Tennessee, she took her single-mom job very seriously but didn't always make enough to support herself and her son. When she woke up one morning and nausea swept over her, remorse hit as she tested positive with her last boyfriend's child. Evie knew that she couldn't abort the baby. Tracie Shellhouse (the director of New Hope Pregnancy Center) guided her through the process of providing life for her baby. With much prayer, Evie decided to put her son up for adoption. After talking many times with the family who wanted to adopt her son, she carried her baby full term, delivered him, and with pain in her heart handed him into the arms of another.

Hearing this story broke my heart. It is true that God has worked Evie's life into good as she is now a police officer and also speaks out to the youth about the severity of gangs, alcohol, drugs, and compromising their faith in God. Evie is also an advocate of choosing life and speaks to young girls everywhere about the power of choosing life and the power of God.

However, I realized that our choices and slight wanderings down the wrong paths have extreme impact on what happens in our future. I would recommend taking some time to read the book Evie has written: Revolving Choices: Playing Roulette with Life. Meeting with her and reading her book has opened my eyes to the world of gangs and the broken and lonely hearts inside of the gangs. My heart now reaches out to all those who are raising children on their own, to all those who have decided to place their children in the arms of others who can give them a better life, and to those who find themselves in a situation because of the small choices they had made. I learned that day that no matter how far anyone thinks they are away from God, God is still pursuing them and reaching out to them with grace and compassion.

Dad's Thoughts
When I look for mentors for my children, I make it a point to try to include people that they just wouldn't seek out themselves, people whose careers or interests may not even be something I personally am interested in. I look for people from different cultures and ethnic backgrounds, too. Because they bring a different perspective on life, my children get exposed to new ideas, new thought patterns and even new ways of doing the same old thing. When you seek out mentors for your children, be willing to let the differences in other people make a difference in your children's education.

Mentors Teach Skills

Most of my life, I have been the type of person my parents' generation would describe as a "jack of all trades and master of none." There are some things I'm really good at, but there are many things I'm capable of doing. I have varied interests and have tried to share those with my children. But my experience is still limited.

Because I'm aware of that, I don't have to be intimidated by the fact that someone else is better at many different skills than I am. I don't have to feel inferior that there are men and women out there who enjoy activities, hobbies or run businesses which are completely foreign to me or don't interest me. But my children might be interested in those things if they were exposed to them.

When I arrange mentors for my children, I intentionally look for people who have different backgrounds and interests in order to provide my children with a broader range of experiences than my own. I was not raised as a hunter and had never really been hunting very much with family or relatives. But Ed McGee is a hunter. For that story, I'll turn things over to David.

My First Hunting Trip
I don't know what was on your bucket list as a preteen, but one thing I wanted to do was go hunting. Most of my friends had been hunting, and they liked to tell sweet stories featuring rattlesnakes, guns, and ten-point bucks. They made it sound like the ultimate "guy" thing to do: a couple of tough dudes with military-grade sniper rifles

sitting in a tree stand, dodging poisonous snakes and trying to avoid freezing to death while deer with racks the size of a small tree walked by every half hour. I glamorized the experience a little, but that's what kids do! It makes the experience more magical.

Anyway, I got pretty excited when I learned that my next mentor, my Uncle Ed, would be taking me hunting. Uncle Ed was (and still is) a spry, fun-loving outdoorsman with a spirit fifty years younger than the rest of him. I knew that spending my first hunting trip with him would be a memorable experience.

Before I could legally kill a deer, though, I had to pass a hunter safety course. I took the online version beforehand to prepare, like the good student I was. The course was pretty common-sense stuff, but I learned how to properly carry a gun, when not to fire it, how to cock and aim, things like that. I needed a 75 to pass and ended up with a 95, since I didn't shoot anyone's eye out, followed all the instructions, and used my brain. I told you, it was common-sense stuff.

Since I was officially licensed to kill, Uncle Ed wanted me to get used to the rifle I would be shooting with and make sure it was sighted in properly. So he took me to a firing range for some target practice the week before the hunt. I had been to a firing range once before when I went earlier that year with another one of my mentors (Week 12, David Cobb), but what's not to like about guns and all the space in the world to shoot them in? I had a blast.

The day of the hunt was a brisk Saturday in late October: Juvenile Hunting Weekend in Tennessee. Dad drove me up to Uncle Ed's house the evening before so I could get as early of a start on the hunt as possible. I slept on the couch in a sleeping bag—boy was I roughing it! I already told you we wanted to get an early start; Uncle Ed woke me up at 4:45 with a flashlight in hand. I've never been so energetic before five a.m. in my entire life.

I got dressed in layers, finishing with a hat and a giant, poofy winter coat—thus proving to everyone present that my mom had raised me well. The sheer amount of clothing I was wearing might surprise some of you, since it wasn't even winter yet, and Tennessee is hardly the frozen north. Let me tell you, if you've ever had to get up at 4:30 in the morning for an outdoor fall sport like I have, then you've seen grown men helplessly shivering on a morning that would later turn into a warm, sunny day. It's amazing how much the sun helps with the whole "warm, sunny day" thing.

The hunt itself took place on a farm that Uncle Ed's cousin owned. He lived a couple of hours away, so we loaded up his old white four-cylinder truck and hit the road. Oh, and we grabbed breakfast on the way there, in case you were curious. I know I sure was curious about breakfast. We pulled into the farm a little before seven, while the sun was still down. A few weeks before, we had set up some reflectors to mark the path to the tree stand, and we used them to make our way across the field and into the trees in the dark. The tree stand was just a little ways inside the edge of the woods. I climbed the ladder, probably twenty feet or so, and sat down on the tree stand's cushioned seat. It was the only part of the stand that wasn't cold metal.

After Uncle Ed left, I got comfortable and took stock of my provisions. I had his scoped .308, a walkie-talkie, and a thermos of hot chocolate whose job was to keep the bitter cold away. I felt like a real man, sitting all alone in that forest: just me, my gun, and the elements. I felt like less of a real man about fifteen minutes later, after I spilled the hot chocolate all over my coat trying to drink it. That was a minor setback, though, and once I got a good stiff drink of cocoa inside of me, the hunt was back on.

Sunrise came and went, bringing with it a dazzling display of colorful hues in the slivers of sky I could see between the trees. Along with the color came the gradual stirring of wildlife: birds chirping, squirrels chattering and rustling, and other animals welcoming the sun in their own unique way. I took a moment during this period of serenity to pray. I remember this distinctly; I didn't pray for a deer but rather prayed that if God gave me a deer, that I would enjoy its meat and not waste its life for nothing.

As I got used to the sounds of the fully awake forest, I slipped into a pattern. I would scan the woods in front of me, check my sides, and then make sure nothing was sneaking up behind me. This was more difficult, since there was a tree at my back, but I managed. After all, it would be unfortunate to get eaten by a bear or miss a twelve-point buck just because I didn't turn around every once in a while. I did this for half an hour or so, showing remarkable patience and focus for a thirteen-year-old, until finally I heard something that wasn't a bird or a squirrel.

About twenty yards to my left and slightly behind the tree stand, a small brown deer slowly paced into view. It had no idea I was there at first, but as I slowly adjusted my body to get a closer look, some sixth sense made it stop and look straight in my direction. Fortunately, I had enough good sense to freeze, because I had read somewhere that deer have bad eyesight and depend more on hearing and smell.

I tried to stay as still as possible. I even tried to picture myself as a part of the tree I was sitting in front of. I could start to see myself blending in with my surroundings, until I was virtually invisible.

Now, you probably don't know this about me since you weren't there that day and I haven't told you yet, but I am left-handed. I also shoot left-handed. In order for me to shoot the deer, which was still below and behind me to my left, I would have to point the gun in the opposite direction from the way it had been resting on my lap, twist my shoulders around, and basically completely rearrange myself in a tiny tree stand, all without the deer noticing. That's no small feat for a young lad whose perception of his ninja ability was far greater than his actual ninja ability. However, by painstakingly inching the muzzle of the gun around until it was pointing in the deer's general direction, and by freezing every time the deer started to get spooked, the plan worked! The deer went back to grazing, and I was more or less in position to take the shot.

I got my sights set on the deer's vital spot, a few inches behind its front shoulder. A bullet there would kill it almost instantly. I had the gun resting on the edge of the tree stand, so I didn't have to worry too much about my hands shaking. There were no trees or bushes between the deer and me. With my target less than thirty yards away, it was a straight shot. I pulled the trigger, and the deer dropped.

All right, it didn't drop immediately. It was obviously wounded, though, and after hobbling around for a few seconds, it fell and didn't get back up. When we finally collected it, it turns out that I hit it almost directly in the heart: a marksman's shot. I killed a deer! I made sure there were no other deer in the area, since they sometimes travel in groups, and then used my walkie-talkie to let Uncle Ed know what had happened. He had heard the shot, of course, but for all he knew, the deer might have taken me hostage and the gunshot was my swift impending doom. He congratulated me on getting my first deer and told me to stay where I was, since it was the time of day when deer liked to come into the woods from the meadow. So, I stayed in the tree stand.

After waiting another forty-five minutes, I didn't see a single thing. Well, that's not quite true. I saw a beautiful red-tailed hawk land just a few yards away from my own perch, and I enjoyed the strangely deer-like rustlings of the squirrels in the underbrush. But I saw no deer. Eventually, my youthful reserves of patience, boundless though they were, gave out and I radioed Uncle Ed to come get me. I was on the one hand excited, since I had been successful in my hunting mission, but on the other hand, I was also a tiny bit disappointed. After all, the deer I killed wasn't very big and didn't have any antlers. What I didn't know at the time is that I hadn't finished the mission; I had just leveled up.

Uncle Ed showed up, walking through the edge of the woods to my right. The sun was fully up, my hot chocolate was fully gone, and I was ready to collect my deer and leave. Fortunately, that didn't make me any less attentive, and as Uncle Ed approached I saw a flash of brown in the woods in front of me. About seventy-five yards out, two deer were weaving in and out of the trees. There was a lot of shrubbery in the way, and the forest floor rose slightly from me to them, so I didn't have as much of a height advantage as I did on my first shot. Uncle Ed, the veteran hunter, recognized the situation almost immediately and silently took a knee close to the base of the tree. His ninja skills were fully developed.

I didn't take the shot immediately after seeing the deer. I couldn't; there was too much cover for them to hide behind as they made their way through the forest toward the meadow to my right. Finally, though, the trees opened up and I got a good look at my target. I decided to shoot at the bigger one first, since I would probably scare the other one off right away. This was a much harder shot than my first success: triple the distance, with faster targets and obstacles in the way. Like I said, I must have leveled up. I got the deer's vital spot in my sights. I steadied myself, bracing for the slight recoil of the rifle, and pulled the trigger! Nothing happened. I had the safety on. Boy, was that a letdown. The only blessing was that they were too far away to sense me and my small movements. I clicked the safety off, repeated the previous few steps, and fired.

I must have been nervous, because I missed my target by a foot. Fortunately, that foot landed the shot right in the deer's neck. It went down briefly, then stood back up and tried to run off. Uncle Ed was yelling, "Put another bullet in! Put another bullet in!" In all the confusion, I had forgotten to reload my rifle and was busy trying to fire an unloaded weapon. Hey, it was my first hunt. I finally came to my senses, got another round in the chamber, and shot the deer again. This time, it stayed down.

Uncle Ed and I were both super pumped. Getting not one but two deer on the first day of the hunting season on my first hunt ever was something only God could have made happen, and I made sure I thanked Him multiple times. After collecting the deer, we loaded them onto Uncle Ed's truck and took them back to camp, where we weighed them. The first one was only a forty-pound button buck, or a buck whose horns haven't started coming in yet. However, button bucks carry very tender meat on them and are great for eating. The second deer was a 110-pound buck: much more respectable for storytelling.

After weighing the deer, we field dressed them together. I use the words "we" and "together" a bit hyperbolically; the reality was that I watched in equal parts fascination and horror as Uncle Ed did all the work. In my defense, I had never seen someone field dress a deer before, and I was very squeamish as a kid. The sight of that much blood live and in person was a different kind of learning experience.

The lesson I learned from my extremely successful first hunt with Uncle Ed was an important one: patience pays off. I could have left after shooting the first deer, and I would have been satisfied with getting a deer on my first ever hunting trip. If I had done that, though, I would have missed an even bigger and better catch. Because I stuck it out and stayed faithful to the hunt, I reaped double the reward, with my second prize being much greater than my first. Additionally, I got to experience a great hunting story firsthand, set up and planned by a master hunter. Uncle Ed's veteran voice of reason and his guidance helped me more than anything else during my time in the woods, and his patience, even when I was ready to go, resulted in a good life lesson learned by me and a lot of good eating for my family.

Dad's Thoughts

How did I feel to hear that someone else had taken David on his first hunting trip where he actually brought home meat for the family? I was thrilled for him. David learned a set of skills from Ed which he wasn't learning from me.

The same holds true for daughters. As a family, we try to focus on teaching our children practical life skills. But mentors can also do that. I'll let Anna share that story.

How I Learned to Change a Tire — in the Snow

I changed a tire in the snow. That's right, the first tire I successfully changed was in the midst of a sudden flurry of white snowflakes. Now, in Tennessee, "flurries" are wimpier than those of the north, but to my thirteen-year-old self it was snow nonetheless. That particular day I had met with Dorinda Beeley, a state-side missionary, wife, mother of two, and member of LightSys Technology Services, an organization that helps missionaries with their computers and technology.

The morning we met, she talked to me about handling offense and potentially offensive people. Some of her advice to me was to not let bitterness and offense overtake me. As a Christian, we are supposed to represent Christ well, and walking around offended and bitter hurts us and the people around us. She walked me through how to come to God honestly and tell Him what the person said or did to offend me, and how to let those things go.

Not stopping there, she told me to be open with the person who hurt me and to communicate with them about their act of offense and how it made me feel. Usually people are just trying to help, not hurt, but in the miscommunication that life brings at times, we don't understand their intentions until we communicate. This is a lesson I am still applying to my life today.

Dorinda also wanted to leave me with a very simple, practical skill; so she drove to a parking lot and taught me how to change a tire. Now that I've learned how to do it,

I feel very capable of changing a tire if one ever becomes flat; beforehand, I would have just looked at the manual and laughed.

Beyond the actual tire-changing process, I learned a few other lessons from that experience. First, if you want help changing a tire, you need to park where the tire you're changing is facing traffic. However, if you're trying to be taught to change a tire, park where people can't see you. Also, do not think that your tire will never go flat when you are driving. You never know when you're going to need to change your tire. So make sure you have the appropriate tools in your car before you're stuck in the middle of nowhere with nothing but a phone with no signal and a jar of expired peanut butter. Finally, if it's snowing and you need to change a tire, try to keep your eyes squinted, as falling snowflakes tend to make the process more difficult if one of them happens to fly into your eye.

Dad's Thoughts
Imagine my delight to know that my daughter had learned to change a tire without me being the one to teach her! She was surprised, too. Something she had never thought about learning was suddenly a skill which had been introduced to her step by step. In one day, she had been gone from a helpless future driver to a young lady with another bit of practical knowledge which, I'm sure, will come in handy in the future. Oh, and she also learned about how to avoid letting bitterness find a place in her heart.

So, in your own planning, look for mentors who are masters at a particular skill. Ask them to share the secrets of that skill with your child. Then watch the results!

Mentors Share Stories

"I had a guy in high school who offered me drugs. I got so mad at him for doing that, that I drew back and hit him and knocked him down. He never offered me drugs again." Those were the words Paul heard during a mentoring meeting from one of the leaders at church. The group of middle school boys was somewhat shocked by that revelation. But it also drove home the point that the man was making in his talk: drugs and alcohol will mess you up badly, maybe for a lifetime. Stay away from them. Don't be around them or around the people who use them.

Everyone likes a good story. Stories are as old as human history. We communicate in many ways, but at the heart of great communication is the story. A good speaker can communicate his three good reasons and get you to agree with him about the soundness of his logic, but a great speaker shares a story which helps the audience to identify with the topic in a personal way. Mentors can be a veritable treasure trove of good stories.

Usually, I drop my children off to spend part of a day with the mentors they meet with. But after developing the mentoring curriculum which we used with middle/high schoolers in our local church, several of the other fathers and I were able to sit and listen to the godly men from our church community who spoke to the group. One man shared how he became the youngest Green Beret in the European theater at the age of 19. He combined his story of expecting to get a big army boot on his backside if he did not parachute jump out of the airplane when the light turned green with the lesson that we have to be ready to go when God opens up doors of opportunity for us.

A man named Roland told the group of boys that he grew up as a backwards, shy country boy who took a zero in his high school English class rather than speak in front of his peers — kids he had grown up with in his school and community. He heard God calling him to be a preacher of the Gospel, but Roland was so sure that God had missed it. Besides, he wanted to see the world, and he was sure that obeying God would tie him down. So he joined the army so he could travel. The result was that he was stationed at Fort Benning for four years and never left the continental U.S. After that, he told God that he still thought He was making a mistake, but he would at least try to be a minister. He unfolded some of his journey as God led him into missions. At the end of his talk, he summed up his story by pulling out a world map with dozens and dozens of pins stuck into countries he has visited all around the globe. God had put the desire into Roland's heart to travel the world, and He had fulfilled that desire once Roland submitted to God's will for him to serve Him by preaching the Gospel. What a story! What a way to visually show these young men — and the fathers — that obedience to God is always the best way.

My daughter Petra got to meet with another Petra who told her some really amazing stories. I'll let her share about them.

Testimonies of Faith
Stories are very important, and they can reveal a little bit about the person. Now, stories can be suspenseful or boring, depending on who's telling them, but the point of a story is to engage the audience and help them to learn

something. Stories can be truthful or they can be a heap of lies. They can uplift a person or tear them down. They can be educational or a waste of time. If you stick with stories—even the plain ones—that are truthful, uplifting, and educational, you'll be labeled as a good storyteller. I want to share some stories with you which I was told by a dear friend and mentor of mine, Petra Setlich. With each story she unfolded, I began to see things in a whole new light.

The first story she told me was about how she a follower of Jesus Christ. Petra was born in Germany and grew up there for most of her young life, but she was not raised in a Christian home. When she was old enough to work, she worked as a bartender. She thought nothing of God and would go get drinks after her work shift. One day, however, everything changed.

It was a normal workday for Petra. She did her job and then went with a friend to get some drinks. The bar they went to was so packed that they had to share a table with some American men from the Air Force. Lonnie, the man she's now married to, was one of them. They dated for two years before he proposed. He wanted to get married, but she wasn't sure about going to America. That's understandable, since she was being asked to leave her country, friends, and family.

Needless to say, they did get married. After the wedding, which was in Germany, Lonnie was notified that his father had cancer. So, three days after the wedding, he left for America. Petra followed shortly after.

She and Lonnie reared their kids for several years before one moment shook their whole lives. One day, one of their children went to a church in town and came home full of joy. Both Lonnie and Petra were very confused at what had happened. Pretty soon, both of their children were going to this church and kept telling their parents about this Jesus.

Since Lonnie didn't want to take the time to see what it was all about, he had Petra visit the church. As soon as she walked through the doors of the church, she felt this unexplainable peace, and tears started to rise to the surface. All during the service, she cried. She cried during the music. She cried while the pastor preached his message. She cried when she went to the altar and got saved. When Petra returned home, Lonnie asked her how it went, and she told him. The next week, he went with her, and he got saved, as well. They began diving into the Bible to find out all they could about God. And everything they read, they believed and put into practice.

One day, Petra was carrying a pot of boiling water next to her daughter. The pot slipped, and scalding hot water poured all over her. Immediately, third degree burns came up all over her daughter's exposed skin. Petra instantly called Lonnie in, and they began praying. Her daughter fell fast asleep, and every single blister and burn reversed and closed up, all except three scabs, reminders of what had happened and what God had healed her from. They believed that God would heal her, and their faith was so great that "mountains could be cast into the sea."

Another story Petra told me was about Lonnie. He broke his arm one day. Immediately, Petra put him in bed and wrapped a wet, thick towel around his broken arm. She called the pastor, and they started praying. Suddenly, as they were praying, the towel became hot, Lonnie's arm straightened by itself, and he was completely healed.

Finally, Petra told me of a story regarding the 32 apartments they used to own. A horrible hailstorm damaged almost all of the apartments, and the cost to repair them was going to be $160,000. A man from the insurance company came and informed them that the insurance policy had changed, so, instead of having insurance to cover all the costs, they would have to pay $1,680 per building. They had never been informed of this change, or else they would have done something about it. They didn't have that kind of money so they did the only thing they could: they prayed. Petra and Lonnie reminded God that they were faithful in tithing and giving, and in Malachi 3:10, it says that He would rebuke the devourer if they tithed. They prayed that He would deliver them from this situation. Three months later, the insurance company called. They said that they had checked and had found no record of informing Petra and Lonnie about the insurance change. The company said that the couple would only be charged $1,000 for the whole project.

When she told me these stories, I just sat there, amazed at God's power. Meeting with her was an absolute blast, and her stories were so powerful. They made facts come alive, helped to build my faith, and gave me a new perspective on different subjects.

Dad's Thoughts

As I have traveled around the world speaking and teaching, this truth has been reinforced over and over again: people love stories. A good story helps to contextualize a principle or lesson. "Does this really work?" "Can it work in my life?" "How did this person overcome obstacles to implement this principle?"

I encourage mentors to share their stories with my children because those stories stick with them through the years. In the coming decades, I have no doubt that my children will pause in front of a friend, an audience or their own children and say, "I remember years ago when someone told me a story" and begin to relate what they learned when they were 13 years old.

As you select mentors for your children, look for men and women who have traveled. Select mentors who have worked with a broad swath of people in their jobs or ministries. Then pointedly ask them to select several good stories to share with your child.

Mentors Influence Spiritual Growth

When I was growing up, I went to school through the week like all the other children. On Sunday mornings, Sunday nights and Wednesday nights, we went to church. On Thursday nights we went to a prayer meeting that my father had started and led. If the doors were open at church any other time, we were there. Then at home, most nights of the week, we had family devotions where we read the Bible and prayed together. In short, I was given a really good biblical foundation by my parents.

That being said, I didn't learn everything I now know about God from them. There have been pastors, evangelists, teachers and even a handful of prophetic types who have influenced my spiritual growth. Some of them helped me to understand more about God's love and grace. Others helped me to realize that this same God demands obedience and a holy lifestyle.

I saved this chapter for last because, well, it's the best possible outcome of mentoring. For my part, if my children grow up to be highly successful business owners, have all the material trappings of success and beat everyone at the game they choose, I would deem my work as a parent as a failure if my children do not know God personally and understand as much as I can help them to understand about His great love for them. This is why I look for men and women of character to meet with my children. It's not enough to be successful in the eyes of a world system. I want my children to meet with people who can reinforce the truths of why we are living our lives each day and how to keep all the facets of life in perspective of the long distance race toward eternity.

One of the women I have had the privilege of knowing is Cathy Payne. To understate, Cathy is a fireball for God. She has graciously spent time with two of my children so far and has impacted many people around the world during her years in service to God. To describe her impact, I asked Anna to share her story.

The God of Miracles

Cathy Payne was one of my mentors who had a huge spiritual impact on me. The day that I met with her, I had no idea that my spiritual life would change so drastically just by hearing the stories she would tell me.

Cathy started by telling me that she was actually a miracle herself. She was born with her face crushed into her shoulder, her legs bowed and her feet twisted upward. Also, she had no nose, and she had severe brain damage. Her dad was angry with God, but her mother told God that Cathy was His.

God began working a miracle in Cathy's life, and each week God healed her a little bit more. Whether it was that she had a nose, or that she was able to move her neck, God healed her so completely that the only thing left in her body to remind her of the miracles of God in her life is that a vein above her eye is out of place and that she has very weak ankles. How about the brain damage? God healed her so completely that her intelligence is actually above average!

These many miracles that she experienced in her life led her to want to share these stories with others and share about the God who did the miracles. After getting married, she traveled with her husband and spoke in revival meetings, she pastored a church, and she spoke at women's conferences all over the world.

God started working through Cathy to heal others, and in one circumstance in particular, the news got out rather quickly. At a women's conference, there was a baby that was so sick that its eyes were rolled back in its head. Cathy prayed for the child, and God healed that baby. Not only that, but the news channel heard about it and came and started broadcasting the conference on live TV! So many people started pouring in to be prayed for that it took six hours for Cathy and her team to pray for all of them. God healed many, many people that day. Cathy went on to tell me about the time she prayed for a lady in Pakistan and saw the cancer drop right off of her. Another man was so close to death that the hearse was present to pick him up; yet, it went away empty because God healed him.

I remember as a thirteen year old listening to these stories and being in awe of the power of God. Yes, I had heard about miracles happening here or there, but this woman's life was a living testament that God is a God of miracles. Listening to her stories raised my faith because she didn't just stop with the story; she also encouraged me to pursue the Lord. She asked me what dreams for my life I had and then told me that God wanted to fulfill those dreams. Looking back even now, I can see how God fulfilled some of those dreams I had as a young teenager and how He's in the process of bringing new dreams to fruition.

What I learned that day simply from being with Cathy and

listening to the miraculous stories opened my mind. I was encouraged in my faith, and I was pushed further in my relationship with Jesus. I have never forgotten those stories, and I have never forgotten the passion and the light in her eyes when she told me those stories. She was someone I met with who was so alive in her faith with Jesus that it made me want to be just like that. Simply one day with her started a chain reaction in my heart to pursue God even more and to ask Him to work through me just like He works through Cathy Payne.

A Modern Day "Brother Andrew"

Have you ever read any stories about a man named Brother Andrew? He was a great guy who smuggled Bibles. Now you may think that there aren't any people left like him, but let me tell you; you're wrong. How do I know? I had a chance to meet with Paul Wang. (Editor's note: Due to security concerns, the name has been changed to protect this man's identity.)

Mr. Wang is a Chinese man living in America. Okay, so maybe "living" isn't exactly the right word. The U.S. is where he has a house and a family, but he travels so much, it's hard to call any place his home. The week I met with him, he arrived from a month-long trip in Japan on Monday, attended a conference on Tuesday, and we met on Wednesday. He knows what country he's going to be in eight months from now, and he's got his schedule all planned out. Constantly on the go, Paul is one big bundle of energy, always at a different place every week. But when I met him, he was calmly working on his computer.

As usual, Dad left us alone after saying hello, and we settled down to business. Dad had wanted Mr. Wang to tell me some of the things he has done in his life, so that's what he started to do. He was born in China and lived there for all of his childhood. However, when he became Christian while working as a Communist interpreter, he wanted to come to a theology school here in America. He didn't think that his superiors wanted their employees studying Western theology in America, but God intervened in a special way. When his boss read the resume, he mistook the phrase Theology for Technology, and approved Paul's trip to the States. He even gave him money for the school, so Paul didn't have to pay anything!

As he got older, Mr. Wang realized that God was calling him back to his native country, but not to live there. He was to be a smuggler for the kingdom of God and carry Bibles to the people there. You may think that in a nation of 1.4 billion people, a few dozen Bibles don't do any good. But in actuality, one Bible alone touches an average of 200 lives! You do the math.

Paul obeyed his calling and has made countless trips to China with friends who are also interested in his work. But don't think it's all fun and games. Not at all; over thirty of Mr. Wang's friends are in jail because of their willingness to follow the Lord. He himself got caught several years ago and was sent out of the country, with all of his Bibles being confiscated. They told him sternly not to return.

Being the follower of the Lord that he was, he came back the next year. However, he was once again caught and was detained for two days. He was interrogated all day and night by five secret service police trying to find out who his superior was. However, the Holy Spirit told him to answer every question "Jesus", as it says in Hebrews 12:2. "Who provided the money for you to come here?" "Jesus." "Who organized your route to China?" "Jesus." So on and so forth. Finally, after they were done questioning him, the police officially banned him from the country for several years and kicked him out.

That just about brings us up to the present. After hearing about Paul's life, I was amazed at his sacrifice and dedication to God. I knew we as Christians are supposed to follow the Lord, but Mr. Wang takes it to a whole new level! When he was done, Paul offered a few tips on how to live life to the best of your ability. The first one he gave me was about how to get closer to God. It was made up of eight things to do differently in your life, and it went like this:

1. Know him more intimately
2. Love him more intensely
3. Trust him more deeply
4. Obey him more completely (Matthew 5:29)
5. Follow him more faithfully (Mark 1:17)
6. Serve him more gladly
7. Please him more purposefully (2 Corinthians 5:9)
8. Proclaim him more boldly (Acts 4:31)

In every single one of those, you are striving for God more each day, and you're becoming more like Christ. Next, Paul told me six individual ways to be the best leader possible, whether on a ball field or in an office:

1. Follow before leading (people will respect you more)
2. Calculate the cost (don't just rush into things)
3. Count the blessing (in everything give thanks)

4. Take the risk (nobody will follow a coward)

5. Assume responsibilities (don't be afraid to admit you were wrong)

6. Pay the price (give even when it hurts)

These traits will allow you to be a general commanding your army anywhere you go. No matter what position you're in now, you'll have more people looking to you for help than you may want.

When Paul had finished giving me these tips, I asked him some questions. First, I wanted to know how and where he met his wife. He chuckled and let me know that they were childhood sweethearts. Now I know this may be hard to grasp, but they both attended the same preschool, middle school, college, and seminary. Obviously, it was a marriage made in heaven. Next, I asked him to share some of the good and bad decisions he has made in his life. Instead of giving me instances, like everyone else, Paul gave me certain circumstances in which he makes his best (and worst) choices. For example, every time he feels the peace of God and finds a biblical instance for his action, he makes a good decision. But the times when his judgment is the worst can be explained in an easy to remember acronym, H.A.L.T.- Hungry, Angry, Lonely, and Tired. Those are the circumstances when he should never make a decision, if possible. Pretty cool, huh?

Unfortunately, the end of our hour together arrived all too soon. I bid Paul Wang goodbye, gathered my things, and left the office of one of the most dedicated, driven, and obedient men I've ever known: a true modern Brother Andrew.

Dad's Thoughts

As parents who believe in a God who loves the world enough to give His only Son, we naturally desire to see our children come to believe in the goodness of God. We want our children to experience their own realization of the Gospel so that "the faith" becomes "their faith." By selecting men and women who are solid in their faith, mentors who have struggled with adversity or great questions but who have overcome them, we are helping our children to realize that this is not just Dad's or Mom's beliefs. It is something which works for people the world over.

Intentions Versus Intentionality

It's very early in the morning as I write this final chapter. The house is quiet. As I reflect on the things which matter the most to me, my mind turns to the opportunities we have in life to help develop the lives and character of other people. For parents, that is primarily our children.

In our culture, we have the old proverb, "The road to hell is paved with good intentions." In the church community, most parents do not intend for their children to grow up and leave the church they were raised in. In the community at large, most parents don't intend for their children to grow up to be drug addicts. The parents of men and women in prison didn't hold their newborn baby in their arms and say, "I really intend for you to grow up to lead a life of crime which will bring shame and dishonor on our family."

Yet, these stories play out every day in the lives of families around the globe. "Good kids" go wrong. They end up in terrible situations, and their parents ponder the question, "How did this happen?" Thousands of books have been written about it. People spend their lives working to help mitigate the results of it. But the basics of why this happens boils down to this question: "Do your intentions translate into intentional actions as a parent?"

One thing I can say with certainty is that my son never would have met with 52 different godly men if I had not chosen to set up the meetings for him. Neither of my daughters would have met with 52 different godly women if I had not taken the time to contact them, ask for their participation and then followed through with the appointments. The middle and high school boys in my church would not have spent nine months listening to stories and life lessons from the men in our church if I had not started writing a curriculum and working with my friend Eric to host meetings in our homes for them. As kind and generous as all of these men and women have been with their time, none of them were seeking out my children to mentor them. I had to initiate the contact.

Each of us has the same amount of time in a day. Some people are more pressed for time due to being a single parent or having to deal with illness in their family. But we generally spend our time based on the priorities we set. If we spend time in front of a TV or computer, it's because we have prioritized that. If we spend hours driving our children to sports practices and spend money on sports camps, it's because we place value on that. If we spend time writing letters asking people to help influence our children, and if we spend time driving them to meet with these people, it's because we have made it a priority.

I hope that during the time you have spent reading this book you have been inspired by what you have read. More than that, I hope that you will take action for your own family. A simple way to get started is to acquire our Parent's Planning Guide. In this book, I go over details of how to start from scratch and build your own mentoring program for your children. Or, if you want to start a small group, you can get the Mentoring Curriculum we have used.

I have spent time writing these resources because I have seen the positive impact in the lives of my own children and the children in our church, and I want to see other children enjoy the same type of growth in their own lives.

But whether you choose to utilize the resources I've written or strike out on your own, do something. Don't just intend to do it. Take action. Write a letter or an e-mail, make a call, send a text message. Start the process of finding mentors for your own children today.

Examples of Mentors

Although occasionally I will ask a mentor to talk about something in particular or do something in particular with my child, most of the time I give leeway to the mentor as to what he or she wishes to do. Generally, that has worked well. You may be thinking, however, "I have no idea what to do with a young person!" So I want to give an extensive list of what some of the mentors have done with my children during their mentoring meetings in order to perhaps spark some ideas of the types of mentors to seek for your children.

Before I begin, I want to mention one thing: not everyone spent time with my children in the context of their day job. Just because a person is a dentist doesn't mean he can't go fishing with a child. If a woman is a home maker, it doesn't mean that she can't take a child for a hike. I have tried to group these by location (Work, Home and Other) in order to give some context as to how and where the mentoring took place. However, not all of the meetings stayed at one location; some were spread out over several locations.

WORK

Artist
One son learned about what goes into making themed environments. The mentor is the owner of a company which uses mostly styrofoam to create artistic and feature-rich environments for children's ministries, dentist offices, assisted living facilities and entertainment parks. My son watched as they worked on a live project, and the mentor even allowed him to help with small tasks.

Missions Director
A lady who spent time with both of my daughters had them job shadow her at her missions office. She shared with them various miracles of healing that she had experienced in her body, including a complete transformation from major deformities she had at birth. Her dynamic personality, her genuine love for people and her single-minded focus on fulfilling the Great Commission made a strong impact on my daughters.

Construction Company Owner
One son spent a day with a Ukrainian owner of a construction company. This particular day, they were building a barn for a neighbor. My son was mostly involved in handing out tools and fasteners; but the overall experience allowed him to see what goes into constructing a barn, and he got to see how quickly that type of structure can be put together when a crew works efficiently. Because the barn is not very far from where we live, whenever he passed it, it was a reminder of what he did that day.

Years later, another son spent a day with this same construction owner, who spent time talking about how he got started in carpentry. He then took my son around the city and showed him different houses and developments he had overseen. After lunch, he let my son work with his crew on the demolition of an attic in preparation for adding more living space. Because of this particular son's love for carpentry, this hands-on experience really excited him about being able to use his skills in a real-world job setting.

Special Education

A woman who works in special education had my daughter spend the day with her. She gave my daughter a good introduction to the children who were in her program and helped her understand the challenges they face. My daughter also learned more about how to interact with special needs children on their level without feeling awkward.

Mother of Triplets

A woman who has adult triplets let my daughter spend the day shadowing her at her job. My daughter helped her on various hands-on projects. She also talked with my daughter about some of the major adjustments and struggles she had to endure throughout the pregnancy and after giving birth.

Radio Station Owner

The owner of a local Christian radio station allowed my son to shadow him and hang out at his offices. My son was able to meet several of the local personalities whose programs he had listened to on the radio. The owner also shared his own career journey with my son and gave him a copy of a book he had written about his life story.

Bakery Owner

A lady who owns a bakery taught my daughter how to do custom and exquisite cake decoration. This daughter already had a business of baking bread for a regular customer base, and spending time with this mentor allowed her to see what doing this type of work full-time would look like. Throughout their day, the lady shared stories from her life, including the challenges of losing her husband in an auto accident and how God restored health to her sons and to her. Even the story of how she started the bakery is a tale of God's direction, provision and faithfulness.

Fiber Optic Technician

From my college friends, I found a fiber optic technician who allowed my son to spend part of a day with him as he spliced hundreds of fiber optic wires in a cable. He showed my son how they cut the fiber optic wires and then prepare the ends by polishing them. He also demonstrated the use of a highly technical tool which he uses to join two tiny strands of glass together in order to service voice, video and data across pulses of light.

Charity Worker

A woman who works at a local charity spent time with both of my daughters during their respective mentoring programs. Due to job loss, sickness or various life challenges, many people in our community have trouble putting food on the table. My daughters spent time unloading pallets of food or preparing bags of canned goods to be picked up by men and women who need the basics for their families. Working with this woman helped my daughters to understand that the people who need help don't always wear worn out clothes. Sometimes they drive a car and have a collar, but they have had sudden changes which have put them on the edge of practical poverty.

Banker

A loan officer at a local credit union met with my son. One important thing he helped him accomplish was to open a basic account that day. He also talked to him about the differences between a sole proprietorship, an LLC and a corporation with respect to liabilities, benefits and taxes.

Lawyer

Good lawyers may be hard to find, but lawyers who are men of godly character are probably even fewer. One such man met with my son and allowed him to accompany him throughout his day. As the counsel for the local government, he had meetings with the mayor along with the county commission as part of his daily routine. Because the lawyer took my son along, he was able to meet leaders of our government he otherwise would likely have never met. He also was able to ask him questions about his career path which included seminary, pastoring, the legal profession and a stint as an educator.

Police Officer

A police officer met with my daughter and shared her life story. She had been involved in gang activity on the West coast, was involved in terrible relationships and had a child out of wedlock. This led to her being separated from her family. Over the course of time and with help from God and her own mentors, she was able to turn her life around. Now, she is able to help people in her own community through her position with the local police force.

Chiropractor

A chiropractor spent time with my son and allowed him to learn about what goes into taking care of the human body in relation to joints and bones. He x-rayed my son and showed him his back structure. He also related an important lesson to my son: your job will have an impact on your own body one way or another. After years of doing chiropractic work, his own body was suffering from the impact of so much pulling and jerking of other people's bodies. He had to close his practice not too long after that simply because he was unable to physically handle the work.

Executive Assistant
A lady who works as an executive assistant for a minister with a national television ministry allowed my daughter to shadow her. She talked about the challenges of keeping his schedule in order and about serving in ways that allowed him to focus on ministry while ensuring that the details got handled. As someone who had done this for years, she helped my daughter to understand more about preparing a good resume, dressing for an office environment and being organized.

Bicycle Shop Owner
The owner of a local bicycle shop met my son for a day. During that time, he watched as the owner fully assembled a customized, short-distance racing bike and then interacted with the customer who came to pick it up and try it out. He learned about different types of frames, wheels, suspensions and other parts; and he was able to spend time looking at the numerous accessories available to cyclists. The owner gave him a good understanding of what it means to be a small business owner, especially in the area of customer service. My son also contributed in a small way by cutting sheets of bumper stickers into individual units which could be given out to customers.

Public Educator
Several local school teachers have met with my daughters

as part of their mentoring program. This gives my children a chance to see what public and private education look like firsthand. A teacher at a private school interviewed one of my daughters as part of her class about the novel she was in the middle of writing. She also had my daughter share with the students her experience of starting and operating a bread business to encourage them in their own entrepreneurial activities.

Office Worker

A woman in our church spent time with my daughter at her work place. During that time, she shared with my daughter the story of how she had become entangled in an affair. Instead of divorcing her, her husband chose to forgive her and to stay married to her; and their relationship is now stronger than ever. Through her testimony, this mentor helped my daughter to understand more about what unconditional love really is, both from the human perspective as well as God's perspective.

Personal Trainer

The owner of a local gym, who also serves as a personal trainer, met with my son. One of the things he taught him was the three things an athlete needs to get to the top and stay at the top: humility, gratefulness and dedication. He took my son through drills he had designed to teach balance and footwork; and because this child was involved in sports, he really enjoyed the skills he worked on that day.

Children/Youth Pastors

Our local children's pastor as well as the youth pastor spent time with my son on different days. Both of them talked to my son about what is involved in being part of such ministries. They talked about what type of work goes into the preparation for the different services they are in charge of conducting. The youth pastor even let my son watch as he prepared his sermon for that night's youth service, which he got to later listen to and enjoy.

Crisis Pregnancy Center Director

The director of a crisis pregnancy center has spent time with two of my daughters at different years. I have asked her to be open and frank about real issues. She has shared with my daughters about the real life and death issues associated with loose morals, sexual promiscuity and decisions made during dating. She also shared some of the stories of girls and women who have been disowned due to becoming pregnant outside of marriage. As someone on the front lines of the battle for the lives of the unborn, her passion for her work was contagious. Both of my daughters still place her among the top five women they each met with during their mentoring program.

Bookstore Manager

The manager of a local bookstore allowed my son to spend some time with him in a job shadow situation. Then, he introduced him to some of his employees who put him to work doing different tasks associated with shipping materials to customers or managing returns. My son got to see the grunt work associated with keeping a retail establishment filled with items. The manager also shared the story of his career journey which was filled with twists and turns.

Local Government Clerk

A lady who works in local government spent a day with my daughter going over some of the details of her job. While she is gifted with service and does her job with excellence, the effect of that day was that my daughter realized firsthand that she never wanted to have an office job like this lady's. Considering how much time and money people spend on degrees without ever knowing if they will like their jobs, I considered this to be a major win.

Newspaper Editor

A newspaper editor spent an entire shift with my son showing him what goes into producing a daily newspaper. Apart from a tour of the place, my son spent a good amount of time watching the editors at work as they prepared stories. When, on a lark, they decided to let the young kid edit a story, he found errors which they had missed. Years later, my son has noted that this was one of the first times that he began to understand that he was particularly good at writing and editing and that those are skills for which an employer or customer would be willing to pay good money.

Dance Troupe Director

The director of a Christian ballet troupe agreed to meet with one of my daughters in a city a few hours away where they were doing a performance of The Snow Queen. My daughter was able to spend time with the troupe taking classes and doing warm-ups before the show. She was able to go backstage and see what goes into producing a ballet performance at an arena. Although she only was able to spend time with the mentor mainly at mealtimes, the mentor opened up her work space and sphere of influence so that my daughter could experience a different world for that day.

Director of Marketing
The director of marketing for a large assisted living facility company let one of my daughters shadow her throughout a day. They attended meetings together and traveled to different facilities. My daughter was able to observe the lady as she listened to a water-related crisis affecting one of the facilities and as she gave instructions on how the staff were to handle it. As someone who immigrated to the United States, she also shared with my daughter some of the tough times she endured because of ethnic tension in her home country.

Widows
Several different women met with my daughters at their jobs or businesses and shared their experiences of losing their husbands through death. Some of them were very young when they were widowed. Hearing their stories of grief, tough life challenges and how they had to continue raising children or making career decisions in the midst of those times was enlightening to my daughters.

Graduate Professor
A seminary professor met with my daughter. She talked with her about pursuing higher education, getting a doctorate and teaching in a post-graduate environment. She also spent time talking about principles of prayer.

Counselor
A Christian counselor met with my daughter and talked with her about the mind. In particular, she talked about how to handle negative emotions in practical ways so that they do not control one's life. She also helped her

to understand how one's thoughts can be a seed that becomes negative behavior. She taught her how to snap a simple rubber band on her wrist to help snap her thoughts back into alignment with healthy thought patterns when they start to go astray.

Financial Tips Editor

One man who operates several newsletters about financial discipline spent the day with my son. He talked with him about several aspects of the proper use of money. One of the life lessons my son learned was that living a frugal life in most areas of life allows a person to afford some large expenditures on a routine basis.

Voice Teacher

A professor in voice at a local university met with one of my daughters who loves to sing. She observed as the professor met with and taught a student. She learned some of the exercises to use in developing her own voice. The professor also shared some of the ways she has been able to use her vocal talent throughout her career and around the world.

Pharmacy Owner

The owner of a local pharmacy allowed my son to shadow him throughout the day at his business. My son participated in some hands-on tasks, such as helping sort medicines. He also learned the basics of what goes into filling a prescription for a customer. The owner also talked to him about some good and bad business decisions he had made along the way.

Geneticist

A molecular geneticist spent part of a day with one of my daughters. As a high-level scientist, she talked with my daughter about some of the reasons she places her faith in God as the Creator rather than in evolution. In preparation for that meeting, I had my daughter contact professors, apologists and other interested parties to gather a higher-level-than-normal set of questions to cover during their time together.

Large-Scale Construction Company Owner
My son spent the day with the owners of a very large construction company. During that time, he traveled to the new airport being built in our area (one of their projects). He learned a little bit about what goes into building bridges, highways and other types of large-scale projects. He also was able to see up close some very large pieces of heavy equipment and to get a sense of their scale compared to normal automobiles.

Pastor's Wife
A lady who grew up in a pastor's home shared with my daughter about having a child out of wedlock. She was willing to not sugarcoat the difficulties she endured during this particular time of her life. In the midst of the shame she was experiencing, she met a man who was willing to marry her, treat her son as his own child and help her grow to the point that she could share a simple story of redemption with other women.

Fire Chief
The local fire chief met with one of my sons and talked to him about his career as a firefighter from the bottom up. They toured the 911 facility so that my son could learn

what happens when an emergency call comes in. During the day, some of the firefighters went out on a call for a burning structure, and my son was able to hear from them about some of the dangers in answering a fire call. This structure had a few thousand rounds of live ammunition which added to the hazards of the smoke and fire. This helped my son to realize that there can be additional dangers beyond the primary emergency.

Scientist
One man allowed my son to shadow him as he worked on a research project for his job. He took him to the site, explained what he was doing as he set up the experiments, talked about the process as the experiment was being performed and then followed up with more details at the conclusion of the experiment. While my son is not as highly trained as the scientist, he was able to appreciate the level of intelligence this man exemplifies in his work.

HOME

Nutritionist
One lady spent the day talking with my daughter about nutrition. Known as someone who leads a healthy, balanced life and who cooks using natural ingredients, she helped my daughter to understand the importance of putting good food into her body. She explained to her the basics of the GIGO (garbage in, garbage out) principle as it relates to the human body.

Gardener
One retired man spent time with both of my sons (different years) and taught them about gardening. One son was able

to use a rototiller and actually dig up the ground. When the other son met with him, due to the weather, they were not able to plow. Instead, the mentor taught my son how to read an almanac in order to determine the best times for planting different crops.

Realtor
A realtor met with one of my daughters and talked to her about how to balance her work with family and her commitment to God. Part of the time was spent at her home, where she talked while folding laundry and straightening up the house.

Years later, this same woman met with another daughter and told her how God had spoken to her and told her to quit her job as a realtor. This actually caused some tension with her spouse who was not completely sure she was hearing from God. However, just a few months later, he was offered a major promotion in another city. By her listening to God and being obedient, she was already in a position to help her family work through the move with much less stress.

Cancer Survivor
One young woman in our community met my daughter and shared her battle with breast cancer. Currently free from cancer, she is living a full life; but she was willing to share not just the physical side of her battle but also some of the emotional questions which arose during this life challenge.

Self-Growth Coach
A former high-level executive in a large corporation spent the day with my daughter talking about various topics

related to personal growth. As an author and teacher, she has a number of exercises and worksheets designed to help young women work through the process of better understanding themselves and their potential.

Welder
A retired man spent time with my son and taught him the basics of brazing and acetylene torch welding over a three-day period. He taught him how to safely work with the tools. He spent time talking about concepts, and then they worked on some basic welding and brazing projects to give my son practical experience.

Photographer
A professional photographer spent time with one of my daughters doing a photoshoot of her. Then she allowed my daughter to use a number of props around her home to create her own still life photos and experiment with her own creativity. This particular daughter has a gift in the area of photography, and this day helped to solidify some of her interest in the subject.

Deliverance Minister
A woman who has had significant experience in dealing with the supernatural talked with my daughters about some of the encounters she has had with demon-possessed persons. She has also had numerous dreams and visions, some of which she has tied into her art (painting, textile and other). Each of my daughters left her home with a canvas which she had painted in the past, a memento of their time with her.

Grandmother

One lady spent time with my daughter at her home and taught her how to make homemade salsa. They worked together preparing all the ingredients, and then they cooked the ingredients until the salsa was to their liking. She then taught her how to put the salsa into canning jars, give them a hot bath and verify that they had sealed.

Retired Missionary
A retired Christian missionary spent time with my son at his farm. They fished together, and he taught my son how to make a rabbit trap. He also shared about his experiences growing up as a child from a very poor family and how his career led him to visit over 140 countries.

Prayer Warrior
One woman spent time with my daughter going over the principles of prayer. Known as a woman of prayer, she shared what she had learned so that my daughter could enjoy prayer at an early age.

Baker
One lady taught my daughter how to make a cherry pie from scratch. My daughter had fun learning how to do the lattice work with the dough on the top of the pie. After baking it, they talked about lessons of life over fresh cherry pie which my daughter had helped make.

Retired Football Coach
A man who had coached football for most of his career in education spent a day with my son. During their time together, he worked with my son on developing his punting and was able to give him some practical tips he could practice on his own.

International Homemaker

One woman who has spent most of her life working as a missionary shared with my daughter some of the practical tips she used to help make a house in another country a home for her children. Some of her tips included developing routines and making sure favorite toys or stuffed animals were always packed for trips. Her oversight helped to ensure that her children were able to feel at home in a variety of cultures and locations.

Missionaries

Several women who have worked as Christian missionaries in different developing countries have met with my daughters. Their unique perspectives on working with families and children in very poor places have helped my daughters to understand more about the real needs which exist in the world. As my daughters have coupled these lessons with their own times spent in other countries, they have learned to appreciate their own opportunities more while learning to be compassionate toward those who do not get to enjoy the same opportunities.

Hollywood Actress

A lady who has had success as an actress in Hollywood and New York talked to my daughter about the challenges she has faced as someone who has tried to live out her faith in the context of a raw and godless environment. As someone who is in the latter half of her life, her insights taught my daughter that fame at any level is not worth compromising your principles and that the end of godly or godless living both have defined rewards or consequences.

Pastor's Wife and Cancer Patient

One woman who was involved in Christian ministry met with my daughter and talked about some of the life transforming events she had in her life. Over the next few years, this woman battled a fatal health problem. As part of the mentoring experience with my daughter, we stood by her grave together for her interment and reflected on her life, her faith throughout the illness and the lessons she had shared with my daughter when they met. Having known her personally, I knew that she would have wanted my daughter to be there as her family both mourned and celebrated the fact that she was free from pain.

Internet Entrepreneur

A lady who is a business owner met with my daughter and talked with her about what it means to be an entrepreneur. She shared some about her business model of doing marketing for clients around the world from her own home. She helped my daughter to understand that being an entrepreneur means being flexible and finding solutions on the spur of the moment. She also encouraged my daughter to find her own unique contributions and to develop them into a business. Now, years later, my daughter has started her own business and is developing it using some of the lessons she learned from ladies like this one.

Mechanical Engineer

My son met with a mechanical engineer who works out of his home. He shared about his experiences of working in large companies, and he helped my son to understand the use of Computer Aided Design software in the development and design of common items used in everyday life — such as cellphones. My son gained a new appreciation for the amount of detail and the type of thought which goes into making common objects useful and available.

Piano Teacher
One of the women who met with both of my daughters is a piano teacher. She has taught piano in her home for many years and remains solidly booked with a waiting list. A very unique thing she did with each daughter was to work through actually writing a song during the day they each spent together. She prompted my daughters on writing the actual lyrics. Then she sat with them and worked through a melody. They then transcribed the melody onto a piece of sheet music. At the end of their day, my daughters each had sheet music of their original compositions.

Politician's Wife
The wife of a high-level U.S. government official took time to let my daughter spend the day with her. She invited her to come while she was having "Nana's Camp," a week of fun for her grandchildren. My daughter got to see how she is attempting to influence the current and future generations by intentionally building character into her grandchildren.

OTHER

Employment Skills Coach
A lady who works with women who are caught in the web of poverty and disenfranchisement allowed my daughter to attend one of the sessions she leads. My daughter listened and watched as she talked with the women about their challenges. She also learned that the women are taught real-life skills such as typing, sewing and such so that they

can better position themselves for employment. The underlying lesson of the dangers of simply going through years of education without learning a marketable skill was highlighted by the plight these women face in their daily lives.

Gun Enthusiast

One man took my son out to a shooting range for some shooting practice. He covered topics related to gun safety and then showed him how to shoot a 9mm pistol. My son had the opportunity to shoot the pistol as well as an assault rifle.

World Traveler

At a family reunion, one of my daughters spent time with a great aunt. This lady talked with her about the importance of listening to advice and respecting authority. She also shared with her stories from her travels around the world.

Cliff Jumper

One of my sons spent time with a man who loves to experience life to the fullest. He took my son to a popular local river destination where there are cliffs and a rope swing. They first did a mild hike and then they jumped off cliffs into the river using the rope swing. My son had a blast. (One of his parents was less than impressed after hearing what they had done.) If you want to do this type of activity, however, you probably should clear it beforehand with the parents in order to avoid an awkward situation after the fact.

One woman took my daughter to a ballet performance of The Nutcracker. They spent time enjoying the performance, and then they had a meal together where she shared her testimony and life experiences with my daughter.

Concert Promoter

My company has hosted the website for a local concert promoter for years. He met with my son in Knoxville the day that he brought in the Chris Tomlin/Toby Mac "Hello Tonight" tour. From 10 a.m. until well after midnight, he allowed my son to roam the premises with an "All Access" pass. My son was able to see what goes on in the preparation and set design for a concert. He talked with security guards and learned that this mentor is the only concert promoter who buys the security guards meals and treats them like human beings. My son talked with the roadies and watched them work. He even talked with one of Toby Mac's band members who ended up taking him onto their tour bus. While he spent very little time with the actual concert promoter, the fact that he provided access to this experience was his contribution to my son's growth.

When my daughter went through the program, the sister of the concert promoter allowed my daughter to spend the day with her when they brought in the Winter Jam concert tour. She gave her an overview of how she helps guide the business side of the concert. My daughter helped the volunteers who were tasked with counting the money brought in from the ticket booths as well as the money received during the offering. It was quite an experience for her to see that side of such a popular concert, and it was certainly the most money she had ever seen in one place in her life.

Conference Attendee
One lady took my daughter to a women's conference hosted by two of her colleagues. My daughter listened to different women share about how to grow in various areas of life. Because of the mentor's connection, she was able to eat at the speakers' table with the leaders. The mentor also bought her several books so that she could help my daughter understand that she should keep reading and never stop learning.

Professional Violinist
A professional violinist spent half a day with my daughter walking along the trails by a lake. She helped my daughter to understand that pursuing a dream or using one's talents on a larger stage requires effort to balance the demands of a career with the time due to one's family.

Scientist/Fisherman
A scientist took my son fishing. While he could have potentially done job shadowing, he spent the time doing something relaxing while talking about poignant aspects of growth and character development. In particular, he helped my son to understand that he did not need to strive to fit in with any crowd. He encouraged my son that it was okay to be different and told him that he should work to be content with being different. At the age of 13, this was an important lesson for him to hear before experiencing even greater levels of peer pressure in high school and beyond.

Author
A successful Christian author met with one of my daughters for a day. She took her around the city near where she lives and talked with her about faith. They went book

shopping to find some books which they committed to read together. The author later shared with me that the day really impacted her in a positive way.

Bodybuilder
One man who has worked as a personal trainer spent the day with my son biking and talking with him about how to take care of his body. At the age of 13, meeting with someone who has a robust and healthy physique can help drive home the lessons of the proper use of weights along with good nutrition.

Bookkeeper
A retired bookkeeper met with my son and talked to him about accounting and about growing up during the Depression era. I had encouraged my son to specifically ask questions about the mentor's childhood so he could hear firsthand stories about what that time was like, which would then impact his view of that time period in American history.

Shopper
One lady wanted to share the life lesson that it is important to have good, clean fun. She took my daughter on a most-of-the-day shopping trip. They went to numerous stores, and she bought my daughter several items of clothing. In between, she talked with her about enjoying life.

Hiker
One of the men who had been involved in children's ministry as a volunteer took my son on an eight-mile hike. During that time, he related how his wife had suddenly left him after seven years of marriage. He talked openly about

how being involved with the church kept him in close contact with other strong men. This forced him to keep in communication and not become a hermit in the midst of such adverse circumstances in his personal life. My son also learned to be sure to take plenty of water on a hike.

Pastor's Wife

When relatives get together, this can be a good time for mentoring. A pastor's wife who was visiting family spent time with my daughter and talked to her about service. She had a set of notes and thoughts she had actually prepared for their day together. They discussed the actions of service as well as the attitude which has to accompany those actions. My daughter told me that the lessons she learned that day really helped her in the way she began to approach even her chores at home. That's always a win.

Widowed Mother

One lady who was widowed with a young daughter met with both of my daughters (different years). She was very candid about the journey her life had taken, the struggles she had to endure as a single mom and the challenges she had raising a daughter in such difficult circumstances. When she met with my second daughter, she took her on their church bus to pick up inner city children for Wednesday night church. It was an eye opening experience for my daughter to see and hear about the types of situations these children have to endure. Both of my daughters learned a great deal from her about dealing with pain and loss and how to overcome life's toughest trials.

Hunter

A relative took my son out one weekend to learn how to

safely use a hunting rifle. Then, on another weekend, he took him hunting. My son was able to shoot his first two deer during this time. He was thrilled to be able to actually bring home meat to put on the table. Historically, this has been seen as a big rite of passage for boys moving into adulthood, and it served as a similar emotional milestone for my son when this happened in his own life.

Tennis Player
A woman who plays tennis spent time with each of my daughters talking with them about beauty and self-perception. Western culture is immersed with plastic people who focus on outward beauty to the exclusion of all else. By talking about this real issue, she was able to bring balance to my daughters and help them to understand that inner beauty and personal character should rate higher than outward appearance.

Pastor
The pastor of a church which has grown from the teens to 2,000 members spent the day with my son talking about principles of growth. As someone who has been a long-term pastor, he was able to share some of the lessons he has learned about working with people and how to use other people's strengths in a large organization.

Funeral Attendee
One of my older relatives agreed to let my son accompany him all day to the visitation and viewing for his deceased brother. He spent time talking with my son about life, death and emotions. This was an opportunity for my son to see this part of the human experience up close and personal.

Acknowledgements

First, I want to recognize my wife Deana who pushed through in the midst of preparing for the coming year's schooling to finish the edits on this book. She has helped numerous international graduate students with their term papers and theses through the years. Thank you for your encouragement and practical support on these books.

This book is one of several which sprang into my mind after a weekend at Rhea Perry's Home Business Conference. Rhea had been after me to write books related to the mentoring program I had been doing for my own children. For several years, I had been thinking about the challenge of getting this material into the hands of other people outside my family. On the way home from the conference, my mind began to teem with ideas for books and projects.

One of those was a curriculum for churches and small groups. While writing that resource, I would get ideas for other books which I believed needed to be written to augment the process. One was this book for parents. Another was a book for the mentors themselves (**How To Be a Mentor for a Day**) and covers the steps an adult can take to prepare for a successful day with a mentee. A third book is entitled **Asking for Wisdom**. This book is written to help young people learn how to ask really good questions so that they get the maximum benefits of wisdom and understanding during their time with mentors.

These books make great resources for parents or youth workers who want something more for the children in their care, and I recommend that you use them together with the planning guide for parents.

About the Author

Craig Thompson has served in various life development and leadership training both inside and outside the US including working with children, youth and adults using public speaking, drama, music and puppets.

His current focus involves mentoring and life development for the next generations. In 2010, Craig pioneered the 52 Godly Men and 52 Godly Women projects with his own children. In 2017, he launched The Mentoring Revolution, a mentoring curriculum for churches and community small groups which is designed to provide an easy-to-use framework for intergenerational training.

He is available for speaking engagements, seminars or conferences.

You may contact him at:

    PO Box 2605 // Cleveland TN 37320-2605

or:

    craig@walkwithgod.com

To support the author's work in leadership development, life training, mentoring and writing more books and curriculum, visit this URL:

https://www.walkwithgod.com/giving

Comments

Did you benefit by reading this book? If so, we would really like to hear from you. To share a comment on this book or a story about how it helped you, send us a note at: mentorforadaybook@thompsonpubishers.com.

Visit us on the Internet at:

    https://thompsonpublishers.com

where you can find more resources and quality books.

Errata

A list of corrected errata is maintained at:

https://www.walkwithgod.com/nurturingyourchild

The publisher requests that any additional errata be sent via the form on that page.

www.ingramcontent.com/pod-product-compliance
Lightning Source LLC
Chambersburg PA
CBHW052104070526
44584CB00017B/2330